D1395478

Halcyon Days

To my wife,
my family,
and my friends

Halcyon Days

Recollections of post-war vintage motoring

by

Rodney Dale

Fern House

First published in 1999 by
Fern House
High Street   Haddenham
Cambridgeshire CB6 3XA

www.fernhouse.com

A catalogue record for this book
is available from The British Library

ISBN 1 902702 05 0

Jacket by Chris Winch Design
Printed in England by TJ International Ltd, Padstow

ACKNOWLEDGEMENTS

Thanks first to my sister Steve Puttick whose recollections and comments have helped to give a more rounded view of events and, as always, to Judith for her wifely support and encouragement.

I am grateful to the following who took photographs all those years ago, and have given permissions and provided information: John Hamperl and others of the Bentley Drivers' Club, David Brooke, Mrs Fish, Tony Gray, Helen Grice, Alec Hodsdon, Mick Jeffries, Dick Joice, Fred Lister, Richard Luckett, Roger McDonald, The National Motor Museum at Beaulieu and its Library, Bruce Nye, Barry Puttick, Dave Rivett, Kent Robinson, Roger Roe, Jack Skinner, Elizabeth Smith, the late John Stanford and his family, David Thirlby and the VSCC, and Paul Wood of P&A Wood.

On the production side, my thanks to Zoë Dale who steadfastly laid out the pages, to Matthew Pettitt and Vicki Morrison who prepared some of the pictures and text, to Claire Bowles for her help and enthusiasm, and to Chris Winch for his jacket design.

Some other books by Rodney Dale

1968 & 1991	*Louis Wain – the man who drew cats*
1977	*Catland*
1978	*The Manna Machine*
	The Kabbalah Decoded
	The Tumour in the Whale
1979	*From Ram Yard to Milton Hilton*
	Edwardian Inventions 1901–1905
1980	*Understanding Microprocessors*
	The Myth of the Micro
	The World of Jazz
1984	*It's True . . . it happened to a friend*
1985	*The Sinclair Story*
1986	(Ed) *Walter Wilson – Portrait of an Inventor*
1988	*Understanding Aids*
1992–94	The British Library Discoveries & Inventions Series: *Machines in the Home*; *The Industrial Revolution*; *Timekeeping*; *Home Entertainment*; *Machines in the Office*; *Early Railways*; *Early Cars*
1995	*About Time*
1997	*A Dictionary of Abbreviations & Acronyms*
	Cats in Books
	Teach yourself Jazz

* joint author

Donald A Dale, the author's father, at work in 1960.

CONTENTS

LIST OF ILLUSTRATIONS

Part 4

Part 1 : PRELUDE 1810–1939

When I started to write this, it was going to be about vintage motoring but, since that part of my life depended entirely on my father's near obsession with motor cars, it seemed to me necessary to first fill in some family background.

In the beginning

My father – Donald Alexander Dale (1908–1972) – was brought up in a strange and opinionated environment. His parents seem to have been ill suited to perform the task of being parents, and were even discouraged from doing so. Alexander Mayo Dale came from a Surrey family of farmers and butchers. Edith Chappell came from a long-established ironmongery family; Alec got her pregnant, and they were forced to marry.

1 — *H. Chappell & Co's delivery van, Bob Dale (no relation) at the wheel. This must have been quite an early Panhard, with its finned-tube radiator and chain drive to the rear wheels. The index mark LB was introduced in 1908. The firm was established in 1834 by my great-great-great-grandfather Henry Joseph Chappell (1810–1891).*

It seems that Edith's father (Edwin Chappell Senior) sought to give the young couple a start by buying them a farm in Surrey, but that Alec sold the farm and made off with the proceeds. Whatever happened, Edith went home to mother, a great Victorian autocratic homemaker.

2 — *Edith Chappell (my paternal grandmother) looking a head taller than her brother (Uncle Edwin) on the 1908 Minerva in a Surrey lane. Was she as fully in command of the vehicle as she looks, or was she getting an earful? Uncle has the Black Dog, and the Minerva has the bald tyres.*

Uncle Edwin

The story goes that the Dales were out looking for Alec's son (why?), so to put them off the scent the young Donnie was entrusted to a nurse, Ruth Neal, and dressed as a girl. His mother Edith became a pharmacist and, like so many other people, found her purpose in the Great War. Afterwards she emigrated to America where you could re-marry without a divorce, and became Mrs Johnson. Young Donnie – my father – heard nothing more of her until he received a letter from an attorney in Kalamazoo (MI) in 1954 demanding that, as her next of kin, he must pay her funeral expenses. In a letter to me at the time, all he said was 'Mrs Edith Johnson's estate has been "wound up".' That was his mother – how sad.

Abandoned by his parents, Donnie was brought up in his grandparents' home, looked after by Ruth; his Uncle Edwin became a father figure to him.

Uncle – 'obviously intended by Nature for a monomaniac' (his words) – was an engineer and mathematician, who joined the Royal Navy to serve in the Great War, and stayed on as an instructor – teaching, inter alia, the Duke of York, later King George VI. After the war, he devoted a lot of his monomaniac attention to his 10-year-old nephew, taking him through the twenties with bizarre correctitude – you should keep your handkerchief in your sleeve, your collar must be this shape, and so on.

3 — *The Minerva photographs, and that of the Humberette (4) were taken with Uncle's Kodak, which produced 5″ x 3″ (postcard size) negatives. I still have the camera, though the alloy backplate has crumbled to a grey powder. The Minerva F38D had a 4-cylinder engine 101.6 x 114.3mm, leather cone clutch and 4-speed gearbox. The chassis was £425 and the whole car £475 (£10 less if you had the 3-speed gearbox). The car has a version of the Roi des Belges body, a style named after the coachwork constructed for the King of the Belgians in 1902.*

Uncle was a Wagner fan; he was born in 1883, the year of Wagner's death – 'the world wasn't big enough for both of us' he used to say – but whether this calendrical *gestalt* was the cause of his Wagnerian fanaticism, I'm not sure. He and my father had to go to the Season at Bayreuth year after year – father so bored that he spent much of the time surreptitiously testing himself for various varieties of BO.

Out of season, Uncle would sit with his clockwork HMV gramophone and Wagner records, calibrating what he believed to be the correct speed of those nominal 78s.

The family – my father, his uncle and his grandparents – was now living in a house called Carnforth in what used to be called Pokesdown, but was renamed East Boscombe because the residents thought Pokesdown lacked euphony.

Various enthusiasms came and went. Always interested in engineering, Uncle invented a new method of making rugs at high speed. He also bought a circular knitting machine to make a special frock for Auntie Nell's appearance at the Bexhill Croquet Tournament. As the tournament wore on, the fabric stretched and the dress became longer and longer, and Auntie Nell's entourage of supporters had to spend much of their time kneeling round her, pinning it up so that it wouldn't drag on the ground.

Another enthusiasm of Uncle's which appealed more to my father was collecting and breeding butterflies and moths, plentiful then in the open countryside. Sometimes it palled.

Uncle (on finding a new caterpillar): 'What do you think this one would eat, old man?'

Father (bored): 'Oh, I don't know. Sausages, I should think.'

Uncle didn't speak to him for three days.

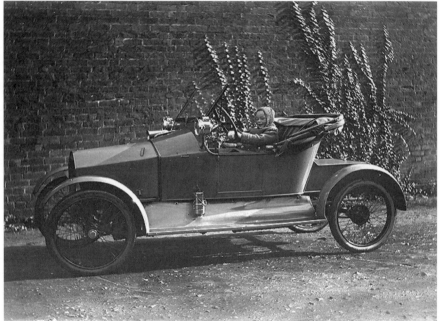

4 — *Father on the 1912 Humberette – an aircooled V-twin with a 7'5"wheelbase and 3'6" track. According to the instruction book 'The RAC rating is 7hp and the licence, which costs £3/3/- should be taken out on receipt of the car, and remains in force until 1st January following. The usual male servant's licence (15/-) has to be taken out for a paid driver.'*

The grandparents died in the mid-1920s. Father and Uncle were alone in the world – Uncle had married in 1913, but sent his wife away after a very short time, because she had assumed (wrongly) that she would be allowed to run her own household. Uncle now found himself the possessor of the family ironmongery business into which his father had put all his energies but, being a naval gentleman, and having a superior attitude to trade, Uncle treated the business as a means to an end, to support his hobbies.

5 — Uncle collected musical instruments, though whether he really played any I don't know. Father occasionally played the piano in the same way as he spoke – in inverted commas. He also played the bass clarinet (which he insisted on pronouncing clarionet) in the school band. Here, he plays a variety of French horn; Ruth is on the soprano sax; Uncle on the trumpet; the flautist is unknown. The picture was taken about 1920.

Blackheath

Father and Uncle moved to Blackheath, and Uncle started to teach mathematics at the Royal Naval College, Greenwich; Father went to read English at King's College, London . . . where he met my mother.

Uncle's hobbies at that time were mathematics, Samuel Pepys, and his private printing press. In 1915, W & R Chambers had published *Chappell's Five-Figure Mathematical Tables*, comprising logs, cologs, illogs, lologs and illologs. In a paper to the Royal Society, Uncle suggested that the contraction 'log' should be 'freed from any taint of slurry': it seems that Napier *et al* had been at fault in producing the unpronounceable word 'logarithm'. 'Antilog' was – er – illogical, so he proposed 'illog'; 'lologs' for logs of logs and illologs for anti-anti-logs. With a flick of the pages of the tables, and a simple addition sum, you can find, for example, that $^{1.406}\sqrt{(1.4123)} = 1.878$.

At 5/- net, Chappell's *Tables* was cheaper than a calculator to do that.

At Blackheath, Uncle proceeded to calculate *A table of coefficients to facilitate interpolation by means of the formulae of Gauss, Bessel and Everitt* and then to set them up and print them himself. OUCH! The work is a formidable undertaking, executed to the very highest standards.

Through all this, Uncle's enduring passion was Samuel Pepys, 'the Saviour of the Navy' on whom he carried out an enormous amount of research. He lectured extensively, and wrote Pepysian articles and pamphlets – many printed on The Press. He also transcribed and edited *The Tangier Papers of Samuel Pepys*, published by the Navy Records Society, with a separate addendum of the naughty bits transliterated into Greek characters.

6 — *Judging by the clothes, this picture of Donnie and Ruth must have been taken at about the same time as that of the orchestra (5). Ruth came as a nurse in 1908 and stayed on as a housekeeper until 1938.*

It was a cruel blow to Uncle that, at Pepys' tercentenary in 1933, the limelight was stolen by Sir Arthur Bryant. I recently heard Edwin Chappell described as 'the outstanding Pepysian scholar of the early twentieth century; far more knowledgeable than Arthur Bryant'. Of course Uncle knew this, and was deeply affronted that Bryant was preferred, but Uncle's spiky personality doubtless lost him votes.

Many years of research culminated in *Eight Generations of the Pepys Family* (1936) in which Uncle documented 890 names of whom 356 were Pepyses, inventing (of course) a genealogical formula to cope with the intricacies.

Estrangements

But back to 1932. Father, having graduated in English from King's College, London, took up a teaching post at Dulwich College Prep School. To be nearer work, he moved to a grotty hotel where he had the temerity to suggest that the waiter might get a clean jacket and that the sugar shouldn't really have ants in it. 'What do you expect for £2 a week?' thundered the manager, 'the Ritz?' Father moved to another grotty hotel.

Being nearer work was only part of it. The main trouble was the Girl Next Door, whom Uncle thought was the ideal mate for Donnie. Donnie had other ideas and married the Girl From King's (History & Economics) in secret.

Celia, my mother (1907–1993), had had a strange childhood as well. Her father, George Hutchinson (1870–1948), was headmaster of Hugh Myddelton School in London; he married a French girl, Lily Delpine, an infant teacher. Lily was not a good mother – 'much too strict and never domesticated'. Instead of showing affection to her daughter, she lavished it all on the poor children of the East End, even taking away Celia's toys to give to them.

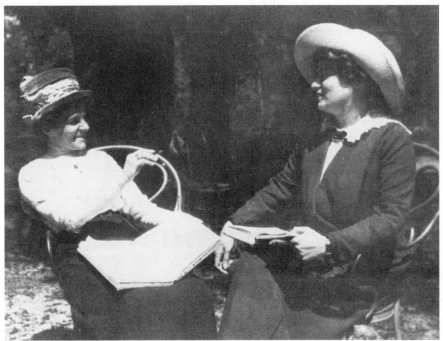

7 — *Lily Hutchinson (left) and Maria Montessori. They became good friends, and Lily acted as an interpreter when Dr Montessori came to lecture in England.*

In 1913, the LCC sent Lily to Rome to attend the Montessori International Training Course, for they wanted to find out more about Dr

Maria Montessori and her avant-garde methods of teaching. Lily went to Rome a sceptic, and returned an enthusiast. She set up Montessori teaching in her own school, at her own expense. Meanwhile, her daughter was being brought up by Miss Adeline Botham, a Hugh Myddelton teacher who gave up her career to look after her.

Came the First World War, and George Hutchinson, who had served in the Bolton Troop of the Duke of Lancaster's Own Yeomanry in the Boer War (bring your own horse and revolver), re-enlisted in the Surrey Yeomanry for the horrors of France. Lily, assuming that he wouldn't come back, sold his valuable collection of books; Celia remembered her mother's rage when he returned unscathed.

Lily continued to work herself into an early grave, dying of pneumonia in 1925. Seventeen-year-old Celia cried 'with relief, not sorrow'; her mother had given her little save the ability to play the piano to concert standard. Her father now married Adeline Botham (1879–1956), known to me and my sister Steve (b1941) as Granny.

Thus both our parents were only children, neither brought up by a mother. They were both clever, though not exactly worldly, people. They were right for one another. Both had fiery tempers, but Father at least mellowed as time went on. He had learned all about obsession from his uncle and, when the time came, he turned it towards collecting ever larger and more impractical motor cars.

8 — *Steve, Father and Ma, with Granny seated, in 1953. Luckily for posterity, the artefacts on the right were not removed and we see, among other things, a bottle of methylated spirit for starting the primus, a box of lighter-fuel capsules, a tin of lighter fuel, a packet of St Julien de luxe tobacco, and a large box of matches.*

Reconciliation

Sooner or later, of course, Uncle had to find out that his nephew had married in secret and, when he did, he was livid, for the Girl Next Door (whom Uncle had vetted as a suitable wife for his nephew) now began to spread vile calumnies about my mother. It was three years before Uncle sent Ruth (now his housekeeper) to vet the household (in 'a mean little hovel in Wanstead', as Grandfather George put it). I was by then two years old. Ruth reported that Rodney was 'a dear little fellow', so we were summoned to The Presence. The rift began to narrow. After a few visits, Uncle confessed: 'I hadn't expected Celia to be so nice'. Well, of course she was. I think he liked me too. On one visit (I just remember it) he gave me a plank of wood, a box of tacks, and a hammer, commanding: 'Write your name in tacks'. Not a bad test, that; I succeeded. Flushed with enthusiasm, I announced:

'I'm going to do it in the floor now.'

'Oh no you're NOT,' said Uncle.

'I think it's time to go,' said Mother.

Uncle may have accepted his family, but to the outside world he was as uncompromising as ever – and why should he reject his principles when he caught someone at the Royal Naval College cheating in exams? He brought the matter to the attention of the authorities, but the miscreant was someone rather well-connected (I have no idea who) and, as Uncle would not resign, he was told that there was no longer a job for him. His loyalty prevented a scandal. He became a naval designer at the National Physical Laboratory, Teddington.

It was on the way to work on 23 February (Pepys's birthday) 1938 that Uncle Edwin collapsed and died in the arms of a porter on Teddington station. His body was taken to Teddington police station.

'Naval gun expert dies at station' said the *Daily Telegraph*.

'The man with bulging pockets' said the *Daily Sketch*.

All the newspapers said that his pockets 'were stuffed with secret plans', actually an innocuous design for a dockyard crane. None of them mentioned that the police gave his sandwiches to a stray dog. It was that which seems to have made the greatest impression on my father.

The end of an era

Uncle, as I've indicated, didn't believe in trade, although H Chappell & Co had produced the money to support his numerous enthusiasms. Father suddenly found himself in possession of the family business, and ill equipped to deal with what we now call personnel management. The family solicitor, and my mother's parents, had long urged that he should have the opportunity of learning about the business, but Uncle would have none of it. As a result, disastrous things sometimes happened. For example, H Chappell & Co used to provide locksmithing services to Harrods and other emporia, and a man was employed to tramp round London collecting the work. One day, Father found him in a restaurant enjoying a well-earned cup of tea, and dismissed him instantly. That sort of thing could happen in those days. When Father told me about it, a year or two before he died, he was very, very upset.

Of course, on inheriting the business, Father gave up teaching (at Davis Lane Primary School, Leytonstone; Headmistress Nellie Gidwell) like a shot. Like Uncle before him, he now found himself with the means of pursuing and developing his own hobbies – at home filling the house with clocks and locks & keys, and in the British Museum studying the lives and works of the Restoration poets Oldham and Rochester (John Wilmot, 2nd Earl of), keeping up the Pepysian research, and writing learned papers on his findings.

To round off the story of H Chappell & Co: the lease of the Fulham Road premises expired at the end of 1940, the goodwill was sold for a few hundred pounds and our connection was severed. Not long after, a bomb fell on it, and it became a large hole in the ground.

Part 2 : CAMBRIDGE 1939–1953

World War II

Chesterton Road

In 1939 we were living in Muswell Hill and it seemed, in spite of Mr Chamberlain's efforts, that there might be safer places in days to come (though in fact 8 Grosvenor Gardens, N10, went through the war unscathed). We spent days touring East Anglia in an old Beardmore taxi, and finally rented *Craigielee* – 142 Chesterton Road, Cambridge – for £80 per annum from the summer of 1939. I was five years old.

It was a toss-up between *Craigielee* and *Tralea* – 3 de Freville Avenue – around the corner. In time, the Mansfield family arrived from Sutton Valence and moved into *Tralea,* and Mickey Mansfield (1934–1983) became my best friend. His father was area manager of Dewhurst the Butchers and drove all over East Anglia and points north in a Wolseley ex-police car EXY938. In due course, Mickey and I sometimes accompanied him, and were introduced to the wonders of places as far flung as Bedford, Grantham, and Norwich. Mickey also brought with him what we always called a trolley; nowadays it would be called a go-kart. This was about the time I'd grown out of my tricycle, going round and round the de Freville estate and getting to know every nook and cranny through drawing maps of the area; now we started going round and round on the trolley.

One of the beauties of 142, apart from its having the attics and cellars which any self-respecting house should have, was the two-storied coach-house at the end of the garden, which provided a double garage opening on to a private lane known as The Lane. The coach-house had an upstairs known as The Loft which I was allowed to use as a playroom, workshop, or anything else I wanted.

Mickey and I spent hours and hours in The Loft redesigning and rebuilding the trolley, and then going for test runs. Once we put a sail on it and went for an exciting speed trial down Haig Road (now Elizabeth Way) – I still have the scars. Only once.

Addenbrooke's Hospital

Not being fit for active service, Father at first thought he would do a PhD in Anglo-Saxon at the University. All I know of his interview at King's was that he *thought* whoever it was he met (could it have been EM Forster?) said: 'How would you like a Bass?'

11

9 — *142 Chesterton Road* – Craigielee. *When we arrived, there were some beautiful railings and a front gate; in due course they were removed 'for the war effort' which was supposed to make us proud to have 'done our bit'. We felt only annoyance, because the railings were dumped behind a row of garages in The Lane which ran behind the house where they stayed until long after the war was over. At that time, Chesterton Road, which had been developed in the 1890s, was lined with beautiful lime trees. Now all are gone – perhaps to obviate the fat, green lime hawk moth caterpillars from falling on people, who might then need counselling.*

'Yes please,' replied Father, thinking they'd reached refreshment time.

'Through there,' said the other, ushering him into a primitive bathroom.

Father made his excuses and left.

For a time he taught English at a school at March, travelling by train, leaving home on a Sunday night and returning on Friday evening. Then the war became more real, and the government sent him to Addenbrooke's Hospital to be a porter instead.

I know that in many ways this was one of the happiest periods of his life. He was doing something in which he found himself taking a great interest: was forced out of his shyness to meet and mix with an assortment of characters who, but for the war, would surely never have found themselves together.

As you will shortly see (about four years in real time) this group provided the variety of expertise needed to get us on the road, motoringwise. One of the group was Jack Skinner, the only one whom I got to know well, and kept up with. Jack was an extremely athletic and creative man, trained as a dancer, and after the war he and his wife Joy developed a speciality magic carpet act – Emerson & Jayne – which they toured until they retired in 1994.

Jack and Father entered into partnership to manufacture handbags which they sold to the nurses and other female staff at Addenbrooke's. This activity took place in the attics of 142, and it was there that I produced my first commercial practical works at the age of ten or so: equipment for dispensing haberdashery, and an illustrated catalogue of the types of bags and purses we made.

Breakers' yards and bus garages

Leather for making handbags was, of course, in short supply so Jack, Father and I took to going to L A Rich, the car breaker in Coldham's Lane, presided over by Les Rich Himself, assisted by Dan and Charlie.

I was in awe of Les Rich – he didn't seem to mind what he said to whom, and it always seemed to make sense. He sat in the first office I had ever appreciated, with a desk deep in papers. The most fascinating feature was a glass-fronted cupboard stuffed full of the old type of folded-card car 'log-books' – hundreds of them. I was impressed also that he wore a pinstripe suit and a tie to work, the colour of the suit chosen to hide the extensive grease marks visible only on close inspection. I went to see him for old times' sake a year or two before he died; the office was just the same, but as an adult I saw the kind and introspective side to a character who had been a small but important part of the jigsaw of my life.

In 1942, a car breaker's yard was wonderfully exciting – what was thrown out in the name of the war effort would make today's connoisseur drool. The point of it for us was the real leather upholstery, and we went up there periodically and did vandalistic things with scalpels. You could get a great bundle of otherwise unobtainable leather for ten bob.

While Father and Jack were searching for leather with scalpels at the ready, I was clambering over and exploring derelict vehicles: not only cars, but vans and lorries – and buses, for which I had a special love; there was something majestic about them in their repose, like sleeping elephants. To board a coach with its marvellous smell, that mixture of oil and musty coachwork, which had come all the way from Scotland – still showing the mysterious word 'Oban' on its indicator blind – and to sit in the driver's compartment was absolute magic.

Mickey and I were interested in all forms of transport, and PSVs in particular – pouring over timetables, plotting routes on maps with coloured pencils, collecting and classifying. After school, we were wont to creep in at the back door of the Eastern Counties bus garage in Hills Road, and revel in the noise and smell of the great monsters being revved up in the repair bays.

Thus we got to know one of the mechanics, Ted Higgins, who explained about bus construction, and maintenance, and on occasion spirited us on board to go out with him on a test drive ('crouch down until we're clear of the garage, and when we get back').

He also introduced us to his brother Jack, an Eastern National driver. EN was the green rival to the red Eastern Counties, and travelled to unheard-of places such as Gamlingay and Mogerhanger, or the heard-of Bedford. One day, we went to Bedford on Jack's bus and, when we arrived, went round to see him as he jumped from the cab. He was all ready for us, and gave us each half-a-crown as extra spending money for the day – riches indeed.

I'd particularly like to remember the Higgins brothers here, because they seem to me now to illustrate one of the profound changes between then and now. So much has been lost with Health & Safety Regulations and what would appear (from the media at least) to be rampant paedophilia that nowadays a couple of responsible lads could never share such mutual enthusiasms with a couple of thoroughly nice blokes – and even to write about it in 1998 seems somehow tainted. I could weep.

Health & Safety would also today preclude the ecstasy of clambering around in Rich's yard. Apart from the considerable number of vehicles in various stages of dismantling, Les Rich also had an early Bullnose Morris and an even earlier Sizaire-Naudin – properly Sizaire et Naudin ('neat, fast and fascinating') – with its transverse front spring unashamedly exposed before the radiator and its enormous central headlamp – hidden under dustsheets in one of his buildings. For some reason he got quite itchy when people crept in and lifted the covers for a peep, an act which I found irresistible, for I'd never seen anything like them before.

Although Rich's was the first, and therefore the best, breaker's yard I visited, there were others. I once found a field down a narrow track off Milton High Street and there, in grass so long you had to push your way through it, was a graveyard of single-decker buses and enormous cars.

Primus inter pares was a Daimler hearse complete with cut-glass bevels and spandrels on the side windows and a spiked rail round the top. As it stood in its overgrown and silent majesty it was the most powerful reminder of the transience of life I'd ever seen. I was never able to find this field again. I would not be surprised if it had something to do with Brigadoon.

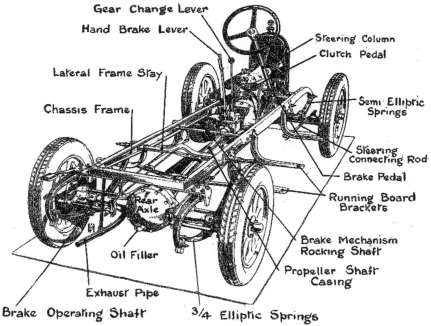

10 — *Morris-Cowley Bullnose chassis. It has a 4-cylinder monobloc engine 69x102mm. The plate clutch has cork inserts and the prop-shaft is enclosed. The car has 4-wheel brakes, and three-quarter elliptic rear springs – a constant source of fascination. Much later, Ed Wilson drew my attention to a Bullnose chassis embedded in a stream at Linton. We put some thought into how to get it out, but the owner seemed to think it was better if it stayed where it was.*

Velocipedes

Father's mode of transport at this time was what was known in days of yore as the velocipede. Just as some people cannot believe that an aeroplane is really held up by those little wings, I think Father was unable – in spite of abundant exemplary evidence to the contrary – to believe that a moving bicycle wouldn't fall over. At first, he overcame the difficulty by buying a cycle and sidecar which I remember as quite cosy though stifling in the sun with the roof on and horrible in the rain with the roof off. The impossibility of balancing on two wheels didn't extend to my mother, for whom he bought a lovely yellow lady's cycle which she rode without falling over, though she did dismount at roundabouts and when buses went past. When I became too big for the sidecar (and sister Steve's arrival in 1941 put paid to rides in the country), Father bought the first of several tricycles. Its main problem was the differential gear – superior to a drive on one wheel only, of course, but useless when not in working order. He spent a lot of effort on trying to get it to work, finally setting the University Engineering Department on to the problem. At last, the differential was set up and continued to function without trouble. For many years, he travelled to and from Addenbrooke's on his tricycle, his hair (long for the times) curling out under his beret, a hangover of life with Uncle, as were the leather body-warmer (as we'd now call it) and the sage green Norfolk jacket. Father was never one to spend a great deal on clothes.

In one of his sorties to Les Rich, he acquired a luggage grid from an Hispano-Suiza which he adapted to fit on to his tricycle. I think that, in Father's eyes, the provenance of the luggage grid somehow lent grace and elegance to the tricycle. The luggage grid could be very useful – as for example when we found instructions for growing mushrooms on one's lawn to help the War Effort. We had enough spawn for six square feet, so Father tied a box on to the luggage grid and went off to Midsummer Common to gather the appropriate amount of horse manure. Although we followed the instructions very carefully, all we got was a solitary mushroom and six square depressions in the lawn which made subsequent mowing very difficult.

Sister Steve remembers Father's luggage grid all too well:
When I was five I started at St Colette's School in Tenison Road, near Cambridge railway station. Father had a luggage grid on the back of his tricycle, a foot or so below saddle. In the very bad winter of 1947 he strapped the body of my old pram crosswise on to the grid, and I was taken to school in this all wrapped up in blankets and with a hot water bottle. I was always warm and comfy but very conscious of the eccentricity of this mode of transport. I was very envious of those who arrived on skis, without a parent in sight. Perhaps that was why I had few friends at school – they feared eccentricity ran in the family. I think it probably does.

During the following blistering hot summer the pram was removed from the luggage grid and I used to sit on a cushion, my legs dangling through the metal bars, and holding on to Father's waist. A slight improvement schoolwise, but not much. Other people arrived on foot, cycled or came on the bus.

Thinking back, I always felt embarrassed about Father, his tricycle and the cars, and the fact that he worked at home. I didn't feel much better about my mother as she had long hair worn in a bun while other mothers had theirs short and often curly. Ours were not normal like other parents, but now I'm very glad they were like that. How boring if they had been like all the others.

The 4$^1/_2$-litre Bentley – OX6934

On its Chesterton Road frontage, 142 was opposite Hallen's showrooms on the corners of Hawthorn Way. When I was 12 or so, I wrote an account of a momentous happening:

We lived with a motor-cycle shop opposite us and until 1944 only glanced at it on passing, but my Father, who was mad on getting a Rolls-Royce, Bentley or Daimler, used to look often in the window.

One day he discovered a chassis in the showroom, a Bentley chassis. He at once made enquiries and paid the necessary money on 5 April 1944. He was very pleased about it and went often to see it. I went too and one day he wished 'to show it to the missus' but he said it in the voice of one who uses the expression as a novelty.

One day as I came home from school at lunchtime, a large chassis was standing outside the shop on the wide piece of pavement. Knowing it to be ours, I went and sat on it, in the hope that someone would come and tell me off. This was probably because I wanted to send the Nosey away with a flea in his ear 'And why not? It's our car anyway.' But no one came, my behind got rather cool and I felt hungry, so I went and had dinner.

When I arrived home from school that afternoon, I rushed to see if the car was there, but it was not. I then went home and was told by my Beamingly Pleased father that he had 'Done 70' on the chassis. Since then if either of us is ever asked how fast it will go we will say: 'It has never been all out, but it has gone at 70'.

OX 6934 was a 1928 4$^1/_2$-litre Bentley and, although it had no body, petrol was unobtainable, and he didn't know how to drive it, Father forked out £125 and the chassis was pushed round into The Lane and into our garage.

Needing a body, where better to go than Les Rich's yard in Coldham's Lane? Father and fellow Addenbrooke's porter Harry Rooke went along to do a bit of measuring, and came back with the news that a 1923 Sunbeam tourer body (£5) would fit the chassis – with a bit of work. We pushed the chassis out into The Lane to await the arrival of the body; it arrived dangling from Rich's crane, Dan the foreman driving, Charlie in attendance. We manhandled the body into the garage and set it in place. Harry Rooke worked out the position of the centre of gravity of the body, and measured the distance from the back wall of the garage. Then he went into The Loft with a brace and bit, transferred the measurement, and drilled a hole in the floor – which I thought was very daring. The hole was, of course, over the centre of gravity of the body; Harry dropped the two ends of a short chain through it, and passed a bar through the loop. Downstairs, he hung a Weston differential tackle from the ends of the chain and anchored the Sunbeam body to the lower block with ropes. I had always been fascinated by pulleys since seeing a diagram in an illustrated dictionary, and the Weston differential in action was very exciting. Up went the body – oh, so slowly (and I can hear the whirr of the chain even now) – until it was as high as the ceiling would allow. We pushed the chassis in beneath, and packed up for the night.

Then began the tedious business of fitting. Night after night, later and later we toiled, lowering the body on to the chassis, marking it, raising it, cutting out a little bit, trying again, an endless iteration until at last it rested snugly on the chassis frame, on what Father always insisted on calling the dumb-irons. Unfortunately, the front end of the body was larger than the chassis bulkhead, but the difference was a consistent $2\frac{1}{2}$ inches all round, so a neat step was fashioned to finish it off.

The neat step is visible in photograph 11 – just behind Father's rolled-up right sleeve – as are one or two other features. At the base of the radiator is a bottle-shaped protrusion which people often assumed to be a supercharger; it is, in fact, the dynamo. Bentley dynamos are smooth; superchargers (on which WO Bentley himself frowned) are finned. You will also see in the photograph that on the radiator cap is a crescent-shaped emblem of polished copper which Father took from the helmet of a Japanese suit of armour he had picked up in the Caledonian Market before the war for a few bob. We were very proud of that crescent, but one day some killjoy pointed out (rightly, but he was still a killjoy) that it was illegal to have a potentially dangerous mascot on a motor vehicle. Father argued that if they got as far as being impaled on the horns of the crescent they'd be in a bad way anyway, but grudgingly removed it. I don't know what he did with it after that, but some 40 or more years later it was dug up in the garden at the Old House, Histon and, not knowing what it was, Ma took it to some 'experts' for identification. They became very excited, and came up with some spurious but satisfying conclusion which I (who hadn't known of its reappearance until then) found very amusing – sorry I can't remember what they said.

Back to OX6934. Father took an old army tarpaulin and a heavy-duty stapler, and soon knocked up a cover for the Sunbeam hood frame. Then he proceeded to paint the whole car – including the hood – silver. One of his theories was that if you painted something with aluminium paint the brush-marks didn't matter, and it was easily touched up. Why, he used to repaint the hood then as some people wash their cars now.

Now it was time for the trials. Petrol was virtually unobtainable, but you could get lighter-fuel if you tried hard. Grandfather George had spent the beginning of the war writing to the War Office, explaining that he'd served in the Boer War, and in the Great War, and that they'd need experienced officers (such as George Hutchinson). Their replies were very kind, but he was nearly 70, so had to be content with looking after the payroll at Short Brothers, who built Lancasters at Bourn Aerodrome. Being a keen bowls player, he joined the Chesterton Bowls Club and, always liking to be involved in something, became the Steward. He was thus able to procure for us a box of those little squidgy capsules of Ronson lighter fluid.

Fellow Addenbrooke's porter Bunty Smith was a would-be ballet dancer – years ahead of his time in hairstyle, for his fair locks flowed down to his shoulders. The only thing I can ever remember him saying was 'That'll do aadmirably,' whether he was handed a cup of tea (and there were plenty of those about), or an adjustable spanner for use as a hammer, or a chisel for use as a screwdriver.

Laboriously we squirted the lighter-fuel into the Autovac; Bunty wound the handle; the engine started instantly. He sprang round into the driver's seat and depressed the clutch – it made a noise like a tiger, which I found very worrying. Into reverse, and the car leapt backwards into The Lane and stopped. It had run out of fuel.

11 — *An early outing to Newmarket. The author sits on the front dumb-iron holding a stick he has just turned into a magic wand by carving a pattern into the bark. The others (left to right) are Lilian and Vic Rayner, Father, Mother and Steve. The photo was taken by Jack Skinner.*

Father climbed on to his tricycle and pedalled off in search of more lighter-fuel. Several cups of tea later he returned, triumphantly bearing two 1/6d bottles of Ronson, and we carefully poured them into the Autovac. Bunty started the engine again; not wanting to risk running out of fuel during a trip to the end of The Lane and back, he drove back into the garage, and that was that.

12 — Now we've all got into the car, and Jack Skinner is sitting astride the bonnet to take this picture. The glass screen that is supposed to shield the passengers is folded flat. It was mounted on hinged arms so that it could be drawn close to the passengers' faces, but we never did because it seemed silly. The body was quite roomy, fore and aft – there were two folding occasional seats in the rear compartment to accommodate me and Jack.

Soon after, limited supplies of petrol became available, on ration at 1/10d per gallon. Buying it was quite inspiring, because our nearest vendor was up Chesterton Road towards Mitcham's Corner: W J Ison (prop Mr Tom Smith). Ison's had a wonderful vintage petrol pump – and I mean pump. On the top of the Hammond Visible Petrol System was a large calibrated glass vessel containing a vertically-adjustable shower head arrangement. You told the operator how much petrol you wanted, and he moved a lever to raise the showerhead to a height corresponding to $^1/_2$, 1, 2, 3, 4, or 5 gallons. Then he placed a hand lever on the square of a shaft protruding from the body of the pump, and pumped it back and forth, whereupon petrol started showering out of the head into the glass vessel. The showerhead contained an overflow pipe so that when the petrol had risen to the preset level it could go no further. Then the nozzle of the hose was unshipped and placed in your petrol tank, and the tap opened, whereupon the contents of the glass vessel emptied into the tank by gravity.

13 — *The Bentley clutch; it is of the inverted cone type where the driven member (with the prominent holes) is pushed towards the viewer by an internal spring, an arrangement which eliminates end-thrust when the clutch is engaged. The pedal operated on the two roller bearings to depress the cone (away from the viewer). This action imitated the noise of the tiger, which worried me – compounded by the fact that the holes in the clutch reminded me of those in the cover of the burnt-out transformer in our old Bush wireless set about which I had had an appalling nightmare.*

Now we had petrol, Father introduced the next member of the supporting cast – fellow Addenbrooke's porter Vic Rayner, who had agreed to drive the car because Father felt a little diffident about it. I seem to recall that Vic had been a chauffeur before the war; he certainly looked the part – a tall, quiet, pipe-smoking, bow-tied man; very kind and considerate. He was the only one of the emergency porters to stay on at Addenbrooke's after the War, moving from portering to medical records.

Vic arrived from Romsey Road on his bicycle. Cans of petrol from Ison's were poured into the 25-gallon tank. The primus was packed, with apparatus for making tea, and sandwiches were built. We were off on a day-trip to Newmarket via Romsey Town to pick up Mrs Vic Rayner. This was the first of many day trips to places such as Newmarket and Ely. I remember that it seemed to take an interminable time to get there (both Newmarket and Ely are less than 20 miles from Cambridge) and even longer to get back. What we did when we arrived I haven't the faintest recollection, but I remember feeling disloyally embarrassed that I found many of our trips somewhat pointless – boring, even.

Sister Steve on family outings

I was about four or five years old, I suppose, when these rural forays began, and they really were rural in those days, even quite close to Cambridge. Vic Rayner had almost white hair and always had a pipe in his mouth, the curling grey smoke smelling sweetly of honey and spices. Even at that age I thought there was something special about the aroma which I could now say was rather sexy.

Mrs Rayner had a picnic basket which she put their sandwiches in, but I can't remember what ours were put in. Knowing Father, it would have been something makeshift – probably an old cardboard box from the Co-op grocer. I got the impression that he hated spending money on household and leisure necessities – but cars were another matter entirely.

Ma's sandwiches were egg and tomato nine times out of ten, but she could never seem to get the mixture to the edges. When the rounds were cut into four little squares [never triangles] there was a luscious lump of filling in one corner, the other three being empty and nothing more than crusts. Still, I ate the crusts first and finished with a delicious mouthful of egg and tomato. For a long time I didn't know you could put other fillings into sandwiches, except perhaps a scraping of Marmite™ (pronounced Mar-meat after the French name for a stewing pot, via our French grandmother). When I first found that a sandwich could contain ham, I was amazed.

We'd park on a grassy verge or turn into a field and spread a rug out on the ground next to the car or at the foot of a nearby haystack. There were lots of small haystacks in those days and farmers didn't seem to mind as long as one behaved sensibly. The picnic was often set out on the running board and we'd take our sandwiches off to a nook in the sweet-smelling hay. There were no drinks cans to cause litter and we always took our sandwich papers home.

Dandelion and Burdock was the thing then; I think one of the most windy drinks ever invented (we called it Dandelion and Burpdock). I remember Father being chased by a hornet – perhaps it had become intoxicated by the fumes from his D&B. How he knew it was a hornet and not a wasp I don't know as I'm sure he didn't stop to look too closely – and why would it want to chase a human being anyway? I thought he was fooling around to make us laugh, which we did, but the picnic ended rather abruptly after that I seem to remember. Hornets are more dramatic than wasps; it would fit in with Father's philosophy – if you're going to be chased by an insect, make sure it's a big one.

There was very little traffic about because of petrol rationing but Father was not one to be deterred from motoring because of shortage of gas. To get petrol coupons you had to both tax and insure a car. Tax was on a sliding scale and the larger the engine, the greater the tax. But the larger the engine the fewer miles to the gallon (or as one wag put it since the cars were old – to the galleon). Other wags insisted on speaking of gallons to the mile – ha ha ha! As time went on, Father got several cars and motorcycles to tax and insure (at great expense) so that he could get lots of petrol coupons, and this meant that even at the height of petrol rationing we could go on reasonably long jaunts. One problem was that you had to have the petrol put into the car whose number was on the coupons, which entailed a good deal of sucking on a rubber tube and siphoning petrol from one tank to another. He had a special metal funnel for sticking into the petrol tank: it had a curved-in flange all round to reduce splashing, and a metal mesh to stop nasties going into the tank. It wasn't long before he found a garagiste who was willing to overlook any discrepancy between the number on the vehicle and that on the coupons.

I don't remember Granny (who had been self-imposedly housebound since 1942) going in the cars at all, except to be taken to vote. Father used to take a lot of old ladies to vote but the problem was you could never tell if they'd vote for the right party or not – the right party being the one which provided the limousine. Was Father given a petrol allowance for this? He must have been; he wouldn't have wasted *his* precious petrol on a lot of old women.

Mr and Mrs Sewell lived out in the country at Ashdon near Saffron Walden. Les Sewell was 'an Invicta man', which meant that he had in a barn two or three 20hp Invictas in various states of dismantling, which he was going to get round to restoring one day. He ran a dull red Lea-Francis shooting brake, as we called them in those days. The Sewells bred ducks, the Muscovy ducks being particularly fine. We had one for Sunday lunch once and Father liked it so much he wanted another one. But this time instead of it being brought to us we had to go and fetch it – and choose a live one from the pen. It didn't taste as good as the first one!

In those days, places which we think of today as just a few minutes down the road seemed miles away and it took an awful long time to reach them. One place we used to take a run out to on a Sunday afternoon was Milton – all of two miles from home! At the beginning of the war, Father had discovered Mrs Bell's stores at Milton where for some reason he was able to purchase almost unlimited numbers of tins of sardines without question. He stored these 'in case of a German invasion' under the floorboards of the front room in the cavity that had been revealed when the joists had been strengthened to bear the weight of the precast concrete air-raid shelter built round our three-piece suite. Father was very partial to a nice sardine.

Mrs Bell did quite well out of Father, especially when she got in a batch of tins of bacon from Poland and sausages packed in lard. It was streaky bacon, rolled up like a wad of fivers. After extraction from the tin, the rashers were carefully unwound and Father loved to fry them and eat them with toast and mustard. The bacon must have been about 70% fat but during rationing it tasted mighty good to those of us who dared indulge.

Father driving

For a time, our outings were dependent upon the good offices of Vic Rayner until Father decided to conquer his timidity and drive himself. Exactly what the history of Father's driving was, I don't know. Uncle had had a Willys Knight in the 1920s, and I presume Father must have 'had a go' on it. His driving licence was dated 1925 (long before driving tests were introduced) when he would have been 17. Moreover, Father inherited the car in 1938; it appears in the inventory of Uncle's estate as 'A Willys Knight Saloon Five-seater Motor car: £5'.

RAC rating & bhp

In those days, cars were taxed on their 'RAC rating'; the horsepower (hp) was taken as being $D^2N/2.5$ where D is the bore (diameter of the cylinder) in inches and N is the number of cylinders. If the bore is in mm, the formula is $D^2N/1613$.

The road-fund licence cost 25/- per RAC horsepower, so the $4^1/_2$-litre Bentley cost £31 per year, or £8/11/11d per quarter, to tax. Later, we found that the $6^1/_2$-litre was £46/5/- and the 8-litre £56/5/-.

In contrast to the RAC rating, the brake horsepower (bhp) gives a more technical indication of engine potency. The engine is assessed at a particular speed (rpm) by running it against a brake. At 3,250 rpm, the $4^1/_2$-litre Bentley engine developed 100 bhp with a compression ratio of 5.1:1 and 110bhp with a compression ratio of 5.3:1.

As I entered a room once, I overheard Granny say '. . . it wasn't Donald's fault the car went into the ditch,' and then everyone went quiet. It was not until I came to write this that I recalled that remark, and it occurred to me that the car Father ditched might well have been the Willys Knight. With Uncle in the background, or the passenger seat, it's no wonder if Father was put off driving for 20 years.

Anyway, he dug out his driving licence and renewed it. Then one day a man (who must have been, I think, some sort of driving instructor) appeared and sat in the front passenger seat and Father drove off – whether or not he knew that I was sitting in the back, I don't know. As we drove along Chesterton Road, the man stood up, climbed out of the car on to the running board, and back into the rear compartment. Then he crossed the floor (it makes the car sound as spacious as it was) and clambered out on to the offside running board. That gave him a different view of Father's driving, but I have never been able to work out exactly what he was doing, except that he presumably thought that he was a helluva guy in some sort of motor rodeo. Eventually he tired of hanging on to the outside of the car, and clambered back into the front passenger seat by the same route. Whatever effect the visitation had, Father thereafter became able to drive.

With this new-found independence, we set off for Felixstowe and a week's holiday in the Beecholme Private Hotel. Felixstowe seemed to be rather lacking in sand, so the beach wasn't that exciting, but we used to spend a lot of time watching other people doing things at the pleasure gardens. Every evening, Father and I would go and watch the roller-skaters going round, and round, and round; as the week drew on I got to recognise many of the faces and gave their owners pet names. I was also fascinated with the big dipper; I never had the courage to go on it – Steve did, once – but I made a detailed study of its mechanisms and it became a close friend. There was also a little karting track, as it might be called nowadays, and this I did have the courage to go on – just the once, because sister Steve who came with me got oil on her dress and we never heard the last of it. We went to Felixstowe every summer for three or four years, and then it lost favour.

Manoeuvres

One memorable Bentley fact was that the $4^1/_2$ had a turning circle of 47 feet, and The Lane was nothing like wide enough for it to be driven into the garage in one sweep. People used to appear from nowhere when Father was trying to manoeuvre into position, and many an 'expert' scratched a triumphant mark on the adjacent wall at which to aim, secure in the knowledge that 'if you go for that, you'll get in third time no trouble'. I'm sure, on mature reflection, that there would have been some mileage (so to speak) if Father had tried backing in, but I don't think he ever thought of it. In any case, the car was too long for the garage so that the doors had to be shut as far as possible and then drawn together with a chain which was padlocked. The rear end of the car presented a much less interesting view than the front, so it was better that way round. Even so, some poltroon squeezed in one night and stole the clock from the dashboard; that prompted Father to have the front knocked out of the garage so that the front of the car would run through into the garden. Then the Scudamore Brothers (Portable Building Manufacturers, Caroline Place) were commissioned to build a shed (of sheet asbestos) on the front so that we could get two cars into the length. And finally, we opened the end of the shed so that we could get cars on to the lawn – to which I will return.

I'm sorry to say that Father wasn't a very good driver. True, he managed to avoid accidents, but he often seemed to be unaware of what was happening outside the car. I remember once on a car journey back from London we came across a newly-tarred stretch of road; Father somehow got on the wrong side of the barrier and we sailed blithely through with men shouting and waving brooms and asphalt forks to speed us on our way. 'Oh dear!' he said.

Most of his cars had very long bonnets, so that turning from a side to a main road could be very dangerous. He took the curiously detached view that, if it was the nature of his car to have a long bonnet, it was nothing to do with him – that was just the way things were. I remember one occasion when he turned out of de Freville Avenue into Chesterton Road into the path of a double-decker bus. The bus driver made an emergency stop and was rightly irate, but made the mistake of asking Father why he had failed to obey the sign warning of a major road ahead. 'There *isn't* a warning sign' said Father, as if that made it all right. He and the bus driver strolled back, and indeed there was no warning sign. For some reason or other the bus driver also seemed to think that it made it all right, and apologised!

Someone once told Father that giving the engine a burst on the throttle would burn the carbon off the plugs, and he translated this into a method of driving where he would put his foot down on the pedal to get a burst of speed, and then take his foot off the pedal and let the car gradually slow down until he deemed it time for another burst. Father's stop–go progress affected some passengers more than others – it made Judith, for example, feel quite ill. The method was much less pleasant in the town than in the country – where it was bad enough. I tried once or twice to suggest modifications to his approach, but without success.

To save petrol Father used to switch off the engine and coast down hill; then let in the clutch at the bottom in an effort to restart the engine smoothly. Of course, if the gearbox was put into neutral the frictional losses were less, but this then required a gear to be re-engaged to start the engine. With a crash (as opposed to a synchromesh) gearbox, re-engagement could be a loud and excruciating problem. The outcome was either success – gliding smoothly away, or failure – grinding to a halt and perhaps using the starting handle to save the battery.

To sit in a car and witness someone using the starting handle can be very diverting; now you see him, now you don't. Father had a special 'tooth-straining face', a bit like a kylin. Down he would go, engaging the handle and preparing for the pull, as it were an athlete about to go for a new personal best. Suddenly the tooth-straining face would pop up, and either the engine would start, whereupon he would leap round into the driver's seat and adjust the controls, or it wouldn't, in which case the process would be repeated.

The Bentley and the Rolls have their gear levers and handbrakes on the right, so entering by the near-side door is often the most convenient route. This may be why Ma took to riding in the back – it would also have afforded Father a better view to the left especially at corners.

Whether by accident or design, Ma gave the impression of Some Grand Lady, especially (says Steve) when she wore her terrible light blue mushroom hat with the veil. Steve took her scissors to the brim, and that

---

14 — In the 1940s and 50s, hand signals were the norm. Some more modern, or modified, cars had solenoid-operated direction indicators and even stop lights, but they were not always reliable. Winkers came in much later, but are not for purists. The official signals are as shown.

I AM ABOUT TO STOP
Extend the upper arm horizontally from the shoulder with the forearm and hand vertical. The palm of the hand should be facing forward.

I AM ABOUT TO TURN RIGHT
Extend the right arm horizontally from the shoulder.

I AM ABOUT TO SLOW DOWN
Extend the arm horizontally with the palm downwards and move the arm up and down with a slow movement.

I AM ABOUT TO TURN LEFT
Extend the right arm horizontally from the shoulder, sweeping it forward with a circular motion a few times.

These spurious hand signals had us in fits:

"I am going to shake the ASH off my CIGARETTE."

"My ARM'S got PINS and NEEDLES."

was the end of the hat. In due course, Ma got a white poodle with a dreadful jewelled collar to accompany her in the back. (Fran)cesca could have been quite a nice dog, had she been allowed.

I mentioned the silvery tarpaulin hood of the $4^1/_2$-litre Bentley, but didn't say that it had open sides. I well remember cowering as centrally as possible, swaying one way and the other to avoid the rain which blew in. However, there were sockets in the body for side-curtains to plug in, so we had a set of frames fabricated at Mackay's, East Road, and clothed by Mr Gentle, the coach builder on Quayside, in the finest rexine and celluloid. There were two problems, however. One was that as the celluloid aged it became yellow; then opaque and brittle. Still, it was better than nothing while it lasted. The other, more serious, problem was that the driver's side-curtain had a little flap through which he could make hand-signals. Unfortunately, however, the size and position of the little flap were unergonomic. Since Father *always* made hand signals, turning corners was a major problem. The right hand was needed for the gear-change – not to mention the steering wheel – yet in anticipation of the hand signal, it was necessary for him to lean over to the left and contort his right arm through the flap, often hindered by many layers of sleeves. The signal having been made, it was even more difficult to retrieve the arm, for the little flap acted as a one-way valve, digging into the sleeve and locking solid. Often, by the time the contraption had been freed, the car had stopped. Eventually, that side curtain was discarded – obvious, really.

As time went on, the celluloid became yellow and brittle. The constant folding and unfolding of the canvas hood caused that to spring leaks as well. But that was much later, when we had several cars from which to choose when we went for an outing.

Additives

At some stage, Redex upper-cylinder lubricant came into favour. Every garage had a Redex can sitting by the petrol pumps, and you added a penny squirt for each gallon of petrol bought. As the description implies, Redex would find its way into the cylinders with the petrol vapour and help to prolong engine life. Father espoused Redex avidly for some time and then, just as suddenly, went off the whole idea.

We spent a lot of time worrying about the 'water bomb'. It cost 15/6d, and you attached it to your inlet manifold to increase the humidity therein and improve performance. Everyone knows 'that time of evening when cars run sweeter', but we could never decide whether or not the water bomb might be worth the investment, so we never got round to trying it.

Poppa's Tipolino – ELB374

Many people got the impression that Father spent all his time 'messing about with cars'. The truth was that he didn't spend *all* his time with the cars partly because he had a job as well. After leaving Addenbrooke's he became a tutor in English at the University Correspondence College, and most days would trike or drive to the UCC offices in the wonderful red-brick-turreted, Queen Anne Terrace, Gonville Place (now under the multistorey car park) to deliver a pile of 'the perishing books' and collect the next lot. Then, having wound himself up to the need to get on with the job, he would shut himself away with his yellow fountain pen filled with red ink, and mark his students' scripts. There was a lot of other work to do; reading set books and setting question papers; unknown to the college, Ma undertook this and found it immensely enjoyable.

When Father had finished enough of the perishing books to assuage his conscience, he would be out with the cars once again, pottering about checking such things as the battery acid, radiator water, tyre pressures and so on but seldom doing anything as advanced as dismantling an engine. I once made a special spring-compression tool for facilitating changing the clutch cone on the Silver Ghost; this was probably the limit of our daring – at least on large cars.

More complex tasks were left to whichever garage was in favour at the time. I'm not sure how Father chose his garages; I expect someone whom he thought he could trust said words to the effect of: 'You want to go to Wallis and Butteau and talk to Mr Stead – he'll see you right', and so it was that Mr Stead at Wallis & Butteau became flavour of the month until something went wrong and it was time for a change.

For some reason, Father decided that the Bentley needed rewiring, and bestowed the honour on King & Harper (popularly known locally as Sting & Sharper) at Mitcham's Corner. So what to do while the car was off the road? He bought a green Fiat 500, ELB374. It was *minute*. According to one description: 'Sliding windows increased the internal room [!!!] and there was ample luggage (or child) space behind the two seats'. I was an early teenager and can testify that that statement is complete rubbish. Even five-year-old Steve found it cramped. For various reasons, we refused to ride in the Fiat, and it disappeared as soon as the Bentley was ready. This, however, was not that soon; because of the second car, perhaps, Father didn't hurry K&H – until, that is, that the roof of the annex in which OX6934 was standing collapsed under the weight of snow (it was early in 1947 – the year of the floods). Father came back in high dudgeon, explaining that the roof beams had been all rotten, and had crashed down on his precious hood frame, and bent it. Thereafter, he took to visiting every day – sometimes more than once – until the job was finished. K&H offered some sort of compensation for the bent hood, and got the job out as soon as they could.

15 — *1936 Fiat Cinquecento (500). The car had a 4-cylinder 20bhp engine, synchromesh gearbox, independent suspension, hydraulic brakes and a top speed of 55mph. The Italians dubbed it Tipolino (Mickey Mouse), a term of endearment rather than of critical appraisal. The company Fabbrica Italiana di Automobili Torino was at first shortened to F.I.A.T., but in 1906 it was changed to Fiat, happily Latin for 'let it be done'.*

The Armstrong Heavy 12 – KV6744

The Fiat having gone, Father chose as his second car a 1934 Armstrong-Siddeley, not Vintage, nasty modern thing. It was black, with the full Armstrong-Siddeley Egyptiana, and the yellowing windows to which we were well used. Triplex safety windows were a glass sandwich with celluloid filling, and would become a deeper and deeper yellow until they were opaque.

Bentleys were on 700 x 21 tyres, of which we had a good stock, but the Armstrong was on 18s, much more difficult to obtain. However, there was a man known as Mr Tyreshoes – I don't think that was his real name – along Chesterton Road by the Tivoli Cinema who was very clever at fashioning treads on smooth covers. Father decided to take up the art; he got out his lino-cutting tools, and proceeded to engrave a fanciful set of tyres for the Armstrong. Off we went to that mystical magnet, Newmarket (in the pouring rain) and – BANG – a tyre burst – the canvas must have been rotten. The wheel was changed and before we'd gone very far – another BANG.

We'd run out of spare wheels of course, so we put the latest burst on the front nearside and sat huddled up in the opposite back corner – bump, bump, bump it went for all of fifteen miles (still in the pouring rain), with people pointing, and shouting such things as: 'You've got a flat tyre'. After that episode, Father was a bit more choosy with his covers.

The Armstrong was a very strange car. Its top speed was about 20mph, flat out down Victoria Avenue Bridge. Cyclists used to overtake it with ease. We could never make out why – 'I don't think it's *meant* to be like that,' said Father.

During the war, there had been a cockney comedian on the wireless – Sid Walker, né Kirkman. (Signature tune: 'Dye ar'er dye, I'm on me wye, singin' ol' rags, bo'uls'n bones, any ol' rags, bo'uls'n bones' – the ' is a glo'l stop.) When he died his son, Sid Kirkman junior, opened a garage in Marlowe Road, Cambridge.

Somehow or other, Father 'found' Marlowe Motors, and it was they who suggested that the Armstrong Wilson preselector gearbox was at fault. Their theory was that the brake bands were slipping. Of course, after months of work, the car was no faster than before. So back it went to Marlowe Motors who overhauled the engine completely, and of course, after months of work, it was no faster than before.

'Oh well,' said Sid Kirkman, trousering the cheque, 'it must be that the car is too heavy for the engine.'

'Do you think they *made* it like that?' asked Father, peering under the bonnet. 'It is rather a *small* engine, isn't it?'

So, making a virtue of necessity, Father donned a mantle of pride at owning a car which defeated the efforts of all motor mechanics to make it exceed 20 mph. He would open the bonnet and display the engine, miniscule by Bentley standards: 'There, look at that. You'd think that they'd be *ashamed* to leave all that space under the bonnet.' At last, Father 'got rid' of the Armstrong. Father always 'got rid' of cars. He often spoke in inverted commas as well, as if savouring a new phrase, or drawing attention to it, sometimes adding – still in inverted commas – 'as they say'.

In spite of Father's considerable support (via the Armstrong) Marlowe Motors went bust. We acquired a nice little portable workbench and a few hand tools, and that was it.

Garages

Those were the days, I should say, when many garages were exactly like that wonderful re-creation at the National Motor Museum, Beaulieu. The country garage had probably been in business since the first motor car arrived in the village, and was largely clad in enamel signs extolling the virtues of long-forgotten tyres, oils and petrols (remember Pratt's Motor Spirit and Power Petrol?)

Every part ever removed from any vehicle was piled up on shelves in case it came in handy. The bench was scarcely visible under the tangle of wires, pipes and tools. There were no electronic gadgets to test engine performance, balance wheels, or align headlamps and steering.

The smell was wonderful – oil and grease; petrol and paraffin; paint, leather and rubber. The men wore grease-encrusted overalls and oil hats. Before the days of hydraulic lifts, legs stuck out from under cars; in advanced cases, there were pits from which to inspect and work on the underside.

There were no frills – you could buy petrol, or have your car repaired, and that was it. It was a long way from self-service petrol, cigarettes, cold cabinets full of food, and gifts to appease the missus after staying out too long with the boys.

The $6^1/_2$-litre Bentley – YF9093

One day Mr Tyreshoes told Father that he knew of a $6^1/_2$-litre Bentley – 'It's at Old Thoday's place, at Jack's Hill'. Father couldn't resist this, and off they went. Jack's Hill is on the old A1 at Stevenage, and Jack's Hill Café was a favourite stopping off point for hungry travellers, especially late at night.

(I remember once ordering there 'sausage potato and onion', a favourite dish. The man laboriously wrote the words on a pad, then turned and shouted 'S-P-O' through the hatch, and threw the paper away. That sort of thing sticks in the mind.)

Old Thoday's place was next to the Café, and built of 5-gallon oildrums filled with earth. In the circumstances, it was remarkably cosy and smelt like the cellar at 142 in which we had spent so many nights at the beginning of the War, before the pre-cast concrete air-raid shelter was built around the three-piece suite.

It was from this olfactorily reminiscent construction that Old Thoday emerged, attempting to straighten a piece of thick wire with a very small pair of pliers, volunteering that he was 'making a bonnet-hinge for an Hispano-Suiza.'

'Oh yes,' said Father. 'Do you have any Rolls-Royces?' I don't know why he asked that.

'No,' replied the other. He paused – 'But I've got some Royces rolled'. He fell about. (I heard later he'd emigrated to New Zealand.)

Then Mr Tyreshoes became proprietorial and showed Father the $6^1/_2$. It was terrifyingly huge, and the criss-cross ash frame of the roof was like a heavy-duty garden trellis and somewhat sinister as it formed a support for adventitious vegetation. The body was filthy, of that faded blue-black colour that bodies like that are, and covered in chicken droppings *etc* inside and out. The car had belonged to Richard Ormond Shuttleworth of Trust fame, killed in an air crash before the war.

Father (to Old Thoday):	How much do you want for it?
OT	:	I can't sell it to you, you're not in the trade.
Mr Tyreshoes (to OT)	:	How much do you want for it?
OT	:	£60.
Father (to Mr T)	:	How much do *you* want for it?
Mr T	:	£80.

And that's how we got a $6^1/_2$-litre Bentley.

Demobbed, champion glider pilot John Hulme had just set up business as a coach builder in Rathmore Road. Restoring the Bentley coachwork was his first job, he told me later, and it kept him going for a few months. When YF 9093 returned, £500 later, she was an imposing battleship grey with blue rexine upholstery of distinctive smell. She was the Standard 6, not the Speed; this meant that she had just one carburettor, with a rather slow response, but made a beautiful noise responding – especially when Father replaced the rotten exhaust system with 18 feet of 4" copper tube from Morlin's.

16 — *The rear axle of the $6^1/_2$-litre Bentley, showing part of the asbestos-wound snake that is the exhaust tailpipe emerging from the top of the silencer and looping over the axle. Note the dinky little oil-level arm on the differential housing. The riveted thing (top right) is the petrol tank, scooped to accommodate the differential housing.*

This was necessary because the original tail pipe rose over the rear axle in a huge inverted U under the back seat, and the top of the curve tended to become corroded as the hot gases changed direction – a well-known phenomenon. When the car came back from John Hulme we all went out for a ride, and those of us in the back felt decidedly ill. At first, Father refused to believe that this could be the case ('Don't be so silly'), but he eventually twigged that we had indeed been shut in a box with carbon monoxide seeping up through the floor – hence the pipe from Morlin's.

The majestic $6\frac{1}{2}$-litre 'Big Six' Bentley had the radiator tapering in at the bottom and a quick-release cap – not to be opened lightly if the engine was hot. I might mention here the whole business of radiator water. The first few winters of our motoring were characterised by the need to drain radiators every night – comparatively easy, once one had mastered the art of (a) finding the drain cock, and (b) not scalding one's feet. When one next wished to go motoring, however, the great copper kettle was set on 'The Ideal Cookanheat' (our coke-fired kitchen range), and other vessels were brought into play, and gallons of hot water were poured into the radiator before the engine was started.

When Father became more daring, he would put some hot water in and then start the engine, topping up slowly with cold water until the system overflowed. At last, of course, antifreeze made its appearance on the market and, after some initial suspicion of this new-fangled stuff, Father espoused it as one of the world's great time-saving inventions.

Topping up with cold water took its toll. We had a wonderful old heirloom: a two-gallon galvanised watering can. Father forgot he'd left this balanced on the front of the chassis after topping up one day, and drove off; he heard a clatter and felt a bump on Victoria Avenue and that was the end of the can.

Steve recalls a similar incident when they were driving along, and there was a great clattering noise. She suggested to Father that the starting handle had fallen off. 'Things don't fall off my cars,' he bellowed. Nevertheless, when he got home he found that he had lost the starting handle (Bentley starting handles weren't fixed) and had to go and search for it. He found it, but never a word of apology.

The $6\frac{1}{2}$ suffered from stuck valves and one day the carburettor caught fire. Grasping the coal shovel with 8-foot handle (left over from the wartime possibility of having to deal with incendiary bombs) that happened to be standing nearby, Father shovelled earth round the carburettor, as though it *were* an incendiary bomb, and extinguished the blaze. All was well.

Luckily there was a little shelf beneath the carburettor, on which he had been able to pile the earth. I returned from school at that moment, and we removed the little shelf and much of the earth fell down. We took the carburettor off; cleaned and reassembled it.

17 — *The nearside of The Speed Six engine showing the twin SU carburettors. The Standard Six had a wonderfully curly manifold with the single carburettor at a much lower level. The curls of the manifold had two little cocks through which petrol could be introduced to make starting easier. When the throttle was opened, the sound of the sucking manifold was like the bath water running away. To the right of the oil filler and breather with its 'B' cap, you can see the starting handle stowed away. To the right of the cylinder block is the tunnel in which, drawing on marine engine practice, WO Bentley's three-throw connecting rods transmitted the drive from the crankshaft to the camshaft. The transverse shaft to the magneto (on this side) and the distributor for the coil (on the other side) is driven from a compressed fibre gear wheel (2:1 ratio) which could, expensively, shed its teeth. The delightful little tank (top right) is the Autovac, which makes use of the engine suction to draw up petrol from the main tank, which is mounted at the rear of the chassis (see 15).*

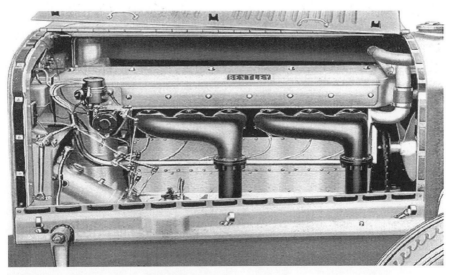

18 — *The offside of the Speed Six engine was generally less action-packed than the nearside. Beneath the coil distributor, the steering box is in the lower left corner, and the steering drop arm emerges below.*

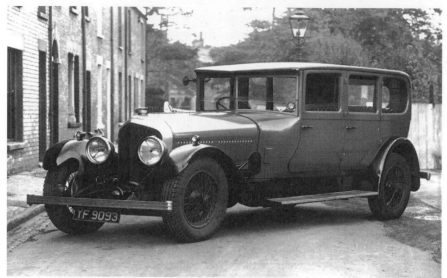

19 — *The Standard Six or 'Big Bentley', as the model was known, before the Speed Six was introduced, whereupon the Big Six became the Standard Six. For those who complained that they missed the 'bloody thump' of the 4-cylinder engine of the 3-litre (unveiled in 1919, and sold from 1921 to 1926), WO introduced the $4^1/_2$-litre from 1927. The pinnacle of Bentleydom was the 8-litre of 1930; the swan-song was that rare model the 4-litre. The body was even roomier than it looks; there were two occasional seats in the rear compartment which swivelled on posts so as to face forwards or rearwards. This sale photograph was taken in Primrose Street by Bruce (Nye). Note the quick-release radiator cap, the Lucas P100 headlamps and the substantial bumpers added by Father. Odd that he had removed the spare wheel.*

20 — *YF9093 as she was when I last saw her (1998), converted to a Speed Six, and with a body reflecting her new image (and everything else).*

'Let's try again' said Father. Again, it caught fire; this time of course there was no little shelf and the earth just fell through. Father took off his coat and successfully wrapped it round the carburettor. Then we cleaned the valves instead.

One of the local wiseacres later told us that when the carburettor catches fire 'you want to rev the engine and that'll draw the flames in and put it out'. Some time later, I had a carburettor fire with my Rover at Caxton Gibbet, so I revved the engine, and that drew the flame in and put it out – I saw it happen.

The $6\frac{1}{2}$ looked so beautiful that Father decided to get John Hulme to do the $4\frac{1}{2}$ as well. I went with John to a yard at Peterborough to look at an Hispano-Suiza body which he pronounced suitable; it was delivered to Rathmore Road and he made an excellent job of fitting it.

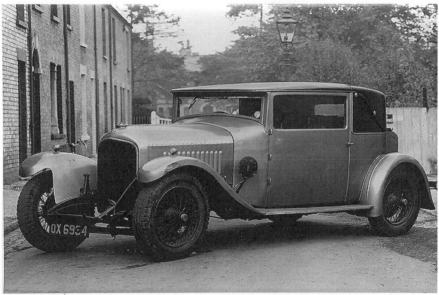

21 — *The $4\frac{1}{2}$-litre OX6934 with her Hispano-Suiza body fitted by John Hulme. The picture was taken at the same session as that featuring YF (19). YF was the lucky one that day; she had the P100s and the bumpers, which fitted OX equally well – indeed, Father would equip whichever car was to be used with these accessories. But where were the spare wheels?*

But in spite of its lovely gold Hispano body, the $4\frac{1}{2}$ lost favour. The close-coupled 2-door saloon seemed claustrophobic after the spaciousness of the $6\frac{1}{2}$ which, even with its folding occasional seats occasionally unfolded, was the size of a small house. So, one day, Father 'got rid' of the $4\frac{1}{2}$. The $6\frac{1}{2}$ lasted somewhat longer – I don't know when Father 'got rid' of it; I had the pleasure of driving it many a mile, and I didn't get a licence until 1951. It probably went some time while I was doing National Service (1953–5). Last time I saw YF 9093 (45 years later) she had been converted to a Speed Six, rebodied, and was anyone's for £300k ono.

Motorcycling

I share two things with Nevil Shute. The first is in counting myself lucky that my youthful years coincided with an interesting technology – in his case, do-it-yourself aeroplanes, in mine, the last days of interesting and elegant motoring for all.

The second thing we share is that our first motorcycles were Rudge-Multis. The Rudge-Multi had a variable-speed drive; the belt between the engine output and the rear wheel ran between two pulleys one of which was made to expand as the other contracted, and vice versa. The control lever swept a quadrant with 19 notches in it on the side of the petrol tank. It was clearly great fun.

My Rudge-Multi was laid up beside the Fort St George, the pub by the river on Midsummer Common, and I used to admire it every day on my journeys to and from school. At last, at the age of 14 or so, I offered the man ten shillings for it – and he accepted; glad to get rid of it, no doubt, for it had been growing into the hedge for some years.

Father kindly extracted it and pushed it home for me – it was hard work because the wheels wouldn't go round. It never ran – it was too far gone with rust for that – but dismantling it was an interesting experience for a young lad. I never even got the engine going properly because the carburettor was missing.

Still, it was more rewarding than the internal combustion engine Mickey Mansfield and I had been planning to build, which ran into problems when our attempts to cast a cylinder from lead demonstrated the vast chasm between dreams and reality.

In spite of the missing carburettor we did manage to get the engine turning. The magneto was suffering from 'shellactitis' as they used to say (though shellactosis would be more accurate), so we baked the rotor in the oven, and it then produced a lovely fat spark. We squirted neat petrol into the inlet pipe and pulled on a rope wrapped around the drive shaft, and it made a few convincing strokes. We decided to call it a day when the rope failed to detach and wound me into the works.

My next motorcycle was an antique 4-in-line aircooled Henderson, which had been used for a simulated-traffic-accident display in Hallen's showrooms which, you will recall, were opposite our house. Father acquired this machine, and we heaved it down the steps into the cellar, dismantled it, and spent many happy hours trying to unseize the engine. We poured hot Redex into the pots, and nothing happened. The Redex cooled. We left the whole thing soaking in Redex for weeks, and still nothing happened. Rust was our enemy, and this machine was doomed as well.

My third motorcycle was another, larger, less antique 4-in-line Henderson EER451 – complete with hand gearchange, offering four forward speeds and reverse. It had lately been used by S H Sparkes, a builder of Devonshire Road, and had a sidecar frame about 5 feet square, which was large. This of course appealed to Father since a sidecar frame – and a heavy one at that – would stop the motorcycle itself from falling over.

The Henderson had been in running order, and was more likely to work than previous machines. However, it seemed to be somewhat erratic, so we got Tom Smith of Isons in to look at it. He fiddled about and one of the plugs fell apart.

'This is stuck with Seccotine!' he said in amazement.

'I know,' said Father, 'I stuck it.' It was the first I'd heard of it.

It looked as if I was going to become a motorcyclist. This didn't suit Father: 'You must have a car,' he said, 'It's safer!' I never told him that I really couldn't see myself riding the Henderson – or, indeed any other motorcycle – because I had a secret knowledge that no motorcycle I owned would ever work anyway.

This machine was acquired by Tony Crosse, of Magdalene, who swapped it for a whole load of exciting-looking but useless ex-WD microwave radar apparatus, much of which has been dogging me ever since.

22 — *The BSA was a very long machine. Among other details, my 1950 drawing shows the acetylene headlamp, the hand pump for oil, the magneto on the exhaust, the primary chain drive from the engine to the separate gearbox, and the secondary belt drive from gearbox to rear wheel.*

In spite of knowing that I was not a motorcyclist, I acquired three vintage BSA motorcycles along the way. We bought the first (EW1217) from Farmer Behagg at Fenstanton for the usual fiver. It was a lovely old machine, in perfect condition except that some of the gear teeth had sheared off, wrought havoc with their compatriots, and now lay exhausted in the remains of the oil at the bottom of the gearbox. We didn't try hard enough to get spares (probably because of the car on the horizon) and the machine was abandoned.

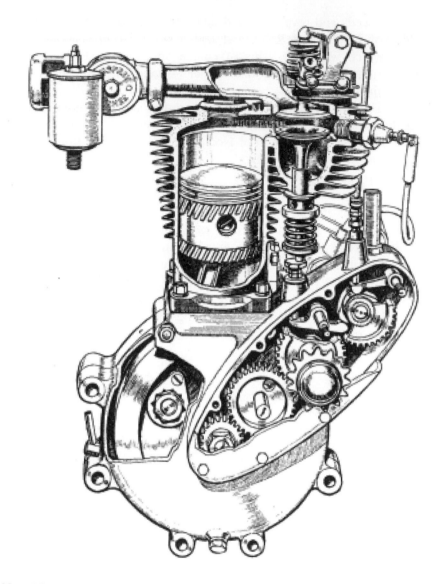

23 — *The Rudge-Multi engine in section, showing a number of features, particularly the overhead inlet and side exhaust valves, and the train of gears – crankshaft to idler (1:2), to exhaust valve cam to inlet valve cam and magneto drive. The engine was started with a small pair of pedals driving the chain sprocket on the exhaust-valve camshaft. It was possible to pedal the whole machine – if the rider had the strength of Hercules.*

I also fell in with scrambler Geoff Wilderspin of Girton at about this time, and he persuaded me that I needed a couple of old mid-1920s Beezers he had lying around – one to restore, and the other for spares. None of this achieved much either, except for the motor-engineering experience and a really beautiful leather saddle of enormous dimensions which I transferred to my bicycle (4/- from the

Milton Road School jumble sale), a 28" lady's machine supplied by the long gone Cambridge Cycle Company of Belmont Place.

Mickey Mansfield, by the way, did become a motorcyclist, and his was the only working machine I've ever ridden. I remember it well, sitting on the heavy, pulsating, maroon Norton one evening in The Lane, letting in the clutch gently – as I thought – whereupon the machine nearly shot away from between my legs. I've never had much of a rapport with motorcycles, and I can't say I'm tremendously sorry.

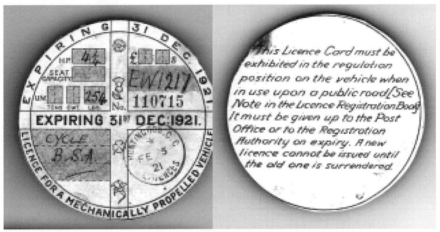

24 — *Strangely enough, for I didn't realise it until recently, the most memorable thing about EW1217 was the Road Fund Licence. It was announced at the beginning of December 1920 that, from 1 January next, all motor vehicles had to carry a licence card. 'Such licence must be carried in a holder securely attached to the vehicle and in a position in accordance with regulations to be made by the Ministry of Transport' (roman mine). It seems odd today that such short notice could be given of such far-reaching legislation.*

The Motor (8 December 1920) made much of the design of the licence holder, and the fact that manufacturers had not been able to produce holders because the MoT had not released details.

By 15 December, a typical DIY article of the period told you how to make your own licence holder from two tin lids.

By 20 December, there was a page of licence jokes: The licence does not bear the owner's name, so the hotel's Head Porter cannot check when 'Mr & Mrs Smith' arrive for the week end (risqué!); on the other hand the man with the apparently enormous car is shown up because the horse power of the single-cylinder motorcycle engine concealed beneath the impressive bonnet will be shown on the licence.

Form RF1, for applying for a licence, was not yet available – that was no joke. Two pages were devoted to the different types of licence holder. The annual licence for 1921 (illustrated above) was to be blue; the first quarter yellow. Subsequent colours had not yet been decided. Fortunately, this example was not handed in as requested.

25 — *The original idea of the rectangular licence was that it could be displayed either in a circular holder, or in a rectangular holder with four windows cut in it. This explains the national emblems in the corners repeated on the vertical stripe, and the repeated expiry date.*

The Rover 8 – HP7707

One requisite for driving a car is a driving licence, and to have one of these it was necessary to be seventeen years of age (which in my case was November 1950). As the time approached it was down Coldham's Lane again to see Les Rich: ''allo, Dale boy, watcher want now? Car for the lad? What about a Rover 8 – lovely little runner – needs a bit of work – 'ave a look *etc etc.*' So for £7.10.0 Father bought me a 1923 Rover 8 which had belonged to the Misses Brown in Sturton Street, purveyors of paraffin. We were all reading Evelyn Waugh's *Decline and Fall* at the time so I called HP7707 'Lady Cumference', shortened to Lady C (long before D H Lawrence was popularised by litigation).

I well remember the day when Lady C arrived in The Lane, hanging on the end of Rich's crane, with, as usual, Dan the foreman driving, Charlie in attendance. At last – my very own car . . . it was Easter 1950, and in a few months I would be old enough to drive her on the road.

26 — *Steel worm and phosphor-bronze worm wheel rear axle drive of the type used in the Rover 8 (and some later Rover models). The underslung design ensured that the bearing surfaces were always immersed in oil; the oil always became loaded with fine particles of bronze as the teeth bedded in, but there was little sign of subsequent wear.*

If you would like a few technical details, the Rover 8 was an air-cooled flat twin of about 998cc, designed by Robert Sangster. It had a plate clutch, 3-speed crash gearbox with reverse, underslung worm rear axle and $\frac{1}{4}$-elliptics all round.

The Motor road test (31 July 1923) extolled the Rover 8: 'A coupé propelled by an aircooled engine and scaling, complete, little more than $\frac{1}{2}$ a ton, represents an interesting combination of economical riding and comfort. It should appeal to the doctor on his rounds, to my lady for her shopping, or her tennis parties, and, with some modification to enable samples to be taken in the boot, to the commercial traveller.'

40mpg and 40mph were claimed, but I think it was more like 50 and 50. Saloon and van bodies were available; the price in 1920 was £300, and in 1924 £145. 17,000 were made between 1920 and 1925, when the model was ousted by the Austin Seven, and Rover went on to the less-exciting 9/20, 14/45 and 16/50.

When Lady C arrived, she was, like the $6\frac{1}{2}$-litre Bentley before her, the dull bluish colour that cars like that are. She should have been on 26 x 3 beaded edge tyres, but they were all crisp and useless.

Easter to November seemed to be plenty of time to give Lady C a complete overhaul and have her ready for the Magic Day. For that, we needed a spacious workshop. Father had a bright idea. He bought a government-surplus barrage balloon, and nailed an old colander on to the top of the clothes prop. With the aid of many ropes tied to the various trees around our lawn, and our faithful old prop in the middle, the colander like a mushroom to stop it piercing the fabric, we built a splendid marquee in which to carry out the work.

The neighbours were wont to make hilarious comments about our erection, to wit: 'What time does the circus start?' – day after day after day. One was a retired farmer who used to regale us interminably with complex and unintelligible news about the state of the Fens at the drop of a hat. Provided that you said 'yes' and 'no' in the right places you could get by, but it could take up a lot of time. The neighbour on the other side didn't say much, but let it be known that he was 'in films'. This I thought was awfully impressive – until I discovered that said films were shorts for the Min of Ag and Fish, showing you how to hold a spade properly, look at turnips, *etc*.

As time went on, the snags in the Big Top were ironed out. For example, one night the whole lot collapsed under the weight of collected rain. We therefore erected a number of secondary, tertiary *etc* poles to alleviate the problem – provided that, during the rainy season, one went round inside, cascading the water from one level to another and finally to earth with the tool provided (a broom with no bristles).

Inside the Big Top, I stripped Lady C to the last nut and bolt and cleaned every part. When she had arrived, the steering box (rack and pinion) was seized up, which was hard cheese. At least, it looked like hard cheese, but proved to be very old grease which I was able to chip away after soaking the affected part in paraffin for some time. The engine was very simple – as I have said, an air-cooled flat twin. I took the pots and pistons to Ted Salisbury at The Hole in the Wall, Cam Road, and for the sum of £4.14.6d the pots were bored and lined, the valves ground, and the pistons oval turned. They don't make cars like that these days.

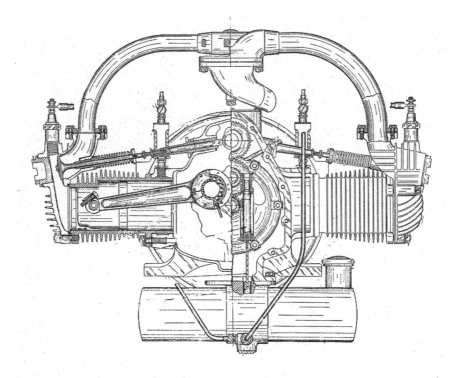

27 — 'An excellent example of the horizontally opposed twin-cylinder engine is that of the 8hp Rover unit.' The aircooled engine is of 85mm bore and 88mm stroke (8.96hp RAC rating). The cast-iron cylinders have detachable heads, held on with three (short) studs in earlier models, and [because of a tendency for red-hot cylinder heads to shoot off into the hedges] five studs in later models. The valves are side by side, with the exhaust valve, and exhaust manifold, towards the front 'so as to receive the full benefit of the cooling draught'. The cast-iron pistons have two rings, and the gudgeon pin has a brass insert at either end 'to prevent cylinder scoring, should the gudgeon pin work loose' o ye of little faith. The necessary fore-and-aft offset of the cylinders is minimised by using roller bearings in the big ends.

The newly-painted chassis frame stood on orange boxes – you don't get those these days either. Young couples of today don't know what it's like to furnish their homes with orange boxes. As I was saying, the newly-painted chassis frame – unfortunately, I used a paraffin-soluble paint by mistake – stood on orange boxes, with the gleaming aluminium crankcase bolted into position. It was a matter of minutes to pin on the pistons, and slip the pots into position. It didn't take much longer to add the combined inlet and exhaust manifold, complete with carburettor. And a couple of sparking plugs were soon fitted and connected.

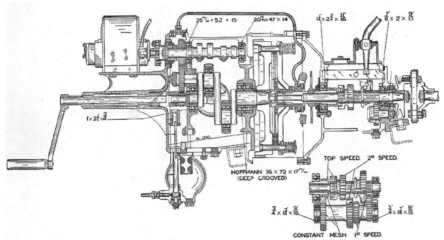

28 — *A sectional view of the Rover 8 engine, clutch and gearbox. The non-detachable starting handle (on the left) is a prominent feature. The magneto (top left) is directly coupled to the end of the camshaft. The round thing under the engine is the cylindrical oil tank seen in section. The sliding-vane type oil pump in the tank is driven by a worm on the intermediate timing gear wheel. The flywheel is keyed to the end of the crankshaft with a Woodruff key. The clutch plate is 8.75″ in diameter. The integral gearbox has three forward speeds and a reverse.*

I filled the float chamber with petrol, retarded the ignition as much as possible, and pulled the handle. Lo! – the engine started. Just like that. The whole contraption jumped about on the orange boxes, and the throttle fell open. The noise was tremendous. I sat on the frame like anything, pretending to be very heavy. How long would a float-chamber full of petrol last? How long would I last? It stopped.

Father came out. 'Did it "go"?' he asked. 'Nearly,' I replied affably. So over the next few days, I reassembled the car, and we would have been ready for a run except that we could only get one 26 x 3 BE tyre. We pushed her down to the garage end of the garden, using planks to prevent the rims from becoming clogged, and stood her on oil drums. My 17th birthday came and went, and still no more tyres. To cut a long story short, we weren't ready to go until the end of March 1951.

Provisional licence at the ready, I stood quivering in anticipation.

The Rover stood in The Lane, ready to go. Now that the moment had come, I felt somewhat embarrassed. However, nobody would know that I hadn't driven before – except Father, and he didn't seem to mind. 'Well' he said, almost testily 'I thought *you* were going to drive it'. So I drove it to Queen Anne Terrace and back – Father sitting silently admiring the view.

29 — *Nearside of Lady C's engine. The five studs (replacing the infamous three studs) on the cylinder head are clear, as are other features such as the magneto, manifold and clutch housing. The anchorage for the quarter-elliptic spring is prominent. There were bonnet sides with generous air scoops to cool the pots, but I never used them.*

It was the Easter holidays, so I entered for a driving test and did a lot of driving. One evening I was visited by Mickey Mansfield and Ed Wilson (who were later to become brothers-in-law, and now, alas, both gone to the Great Workshop in the Sky). They wanted a ride in the Rover, so Father came along to act as the Authorised Accompanist and Mickey and Ed sat in the dickey seat. The unladen weight of the car was only about 10cwt, so the addition of two grown lads over the rear axle had a dramatically negative effect on the brakes which I didn't discover until trying to stop at the traffic lights in Chesterton Lane, where I ran into the back of another car with a mighty 'wump'. Oddly enough, instead of getting out to see what had happened, the driver sped away like a scalded cat – 'up to no good', we concluded.

Lady C was making a tremendous noise because the engine hadn't stopped and Father's sympathetic brake application had pushed a floorboard out, and it had jammed the clutch pedal down. We untangled the board and went home slowly; the offside end of the front axle was severely bent. Father took it to George Lister in Abbey Road, who straightened it for ten bob.

30 — *Underside of Lady C viewed from the rear; the worm housing is prominent. The 4-spoke wheel on the right is the speedometer drive, driven by a belt round the prop-shaft. I adjusted the ratio by winding a strip of balloon fabric round the prop-shaft until the speedometer reading became plausible, and then securing it with a couple of jubilee clips.*

Someone said that to facilitate passing the driving test it would be a good idea to have a driving lesson, because the instructors knew all about the routes used, the questions asked, and so on, so I went to Marshall's in Jesus Lane and booked a couple – 7/6d each. Mr Franklin of Marshalls – who later set up his own driving school in Tennis Court Road – took me round the test routes, and questioned me on the highway code. Came the day of the test. No examination before or since has worried me more – I couldn't eat a thing for lunch. Another adviser had suggested that it was good practice to book a test in the afternoon, in the hope that the tester himself had had a good lunch. It was at 2.30, and went like a dream – until, in Bateman Street, we did an emergency stop. That was all right, because when the tester looked behind, you knew that he was going to shout 'stop!' However: 'Reverse into there,' commanded Mr Langford, indicating St Eligius Street, which is very narrow. As I began the manoeuvre, I noted that a dustcart was coming out, which rattled me. The hind wheel went up on the pavement, so I knew that I'd failed. 'Oh bugger – Sir' I shouted, because I knew I'd failed. 'Right,' he said, 'let's go back'. We did, and he asked me some questions about the highway code. 'Thank you very much,' he said, scribbling a bit of paper to say that I'd passed. It must have been because I'd called him Sir. They don't make tests like that these days.

Father and I went to the Shire Hall to convert my provisional licence, and then I drove home. We got out, spread the glad tidings, and I got in again.

'Where are you going?' asked Father.

'For a drive on my own,' I said.

'I'd have thought you'd have had enough of driving,' he said. But is there anything as joyous as one's first solo?

31 — *Lady C on an early outing – on the way back from the Festival of Britain in 1951. The windscreen and hood come from a Triumph at Rich's. The mudguards are fashioned from the bonnet of the Hispano-Suiza whose body had clothed the 4$^1/_2$-litre Bentley. The piece of angle iron strengthening the construction and carrying the headlamps is from an old bedframe. The spare wheel is supported only on its central post – rather a strain for the post, but I later added running boards, which helped to support it. The dickey seat is open, as is the passenger's door (the driver had no door, and had to climb over, or slide across). The passenger is Richard Duke, who is saying: 'There goes the fox!' for the nth time, which may be why I look somewhat jaded.*

HP7707 was jade green, and it used to cost 1/6 to repaint her. This was for a tin of Brushing Belco, which Father averred was formulated so that the brush marks disappeared – the bristles of the brush, so the story went, laid paint in the grooves left from the previous application. Since it didn't seem to work, and I believed what Father said, I couldn't help thinking that there was something wrong with my technique. Anyway, it didn't matter, because I was wont to paint her quite often, hoping that the troughs this time would coincide with the peaks last time. She lacked a windscreen and hood, but Father very cleverly adapted a screen and frame from an old Triumph (10/- from Les Rich) and made a canvas cover for it. He was very good at that sort of thing.

I passed my test at the end of May 1951, and almost immediately decided to tour Cornwall with two school friends: Mick Jefferies and Roger Roe. None of us had had to organise a trip such as this before, and we spent a great deal of time poring over maps, deciding what route we should take, where we should stop for the night and so on. For a time I wondered whether we should take a spare engine with us, but dissuaded myself when logic dictated that, if a spare engine, why not a whole spare car? The idea of towing a complete chassis in case of breakdown – and we seriously considered this – became even more ludicrous when I realised that, if some part vital to mobility, such as a wheel bearing, had to be changed, we'd really be in it.

Then, where to stow all our kit? The final arrangement was an extended ammunition box on the off side, and a frame to lay across the open dickey seat to take a kit bag on each side (**32**). It all worked perfectly, and there was no mechanical trouble apart from a puncture which I repaired literally in a couple of minutes at St Austell.

I had been awarded a scholarship to Cambridge on my Higher Certificate results in 1950, but nobody suggested that I should leave school (The Perse, when it was opposite the Catholic Church in Hills Road) and do something useful.

The school was a mechanism for outputting boys to the university, which meant Cambridge, although Oxford was OK as well. 'Oily' Hawkins interviewed me on one of the grand pianos in the School Hall (using it as a table, you understand). 'Which college are you going to?' 'I don't know, Sir.' 'We haven't had anyone at Queens' recently.' So I had an interview at Queens' College, and got my place.

Then, rather than broadening my horizons, I stayed on and on at school until at last they *had* to make me a prefect. I used to drive to school in Lady C and park in Harvey Road and nip over the wall donning the obligatory school cap to turn into a schoolboy. Headmaster Stanley Stubbs – who had confessed to my parents that he didn't understand me (although most of us thought that he didn't understand boys full stop) – expressed concern in Assembly that some boys were coming to school on motor cycles, which were dangerous. He then uttered the immortal words: 'Save your money and buy a little car.' Perhaps he knew about Lady C after all, though he never tackled me about her. I eventually left school at Christmas 1952, having filled in the time by taking A-level chemistry, zoology, botany and the general paper two years running. What a waste of time.

32 — *The 1951 Cornish Tour. Mick Jeffries (left) and I packing up at Sutton Scotney after our first night's stay. There is a kit-bag on each side of the open dickey-seat.*

33 — *Those were the days. And so much cheaper to run than barbed wire, tunnels,* etc.

34 — *Mick at Stonehenge – the duffel coat comes into its own.*

35 — *Waking up at Moretonhampstead, Devon.*

36 — *Clarabelle, as we called her, at Grampound, Cornwall, on the A390. She wouldn't let us put up our tent in her field, so we put it up in her shed and parked across the doorway. She wasn't best pleased.*

37 — *Mick in Clarabelle's shed, watching the pot boiling on our faithful primus.*

38 — *Lady C arrives at Land's End, and immediately attracts a crowd. Mick in his duffel coat is on the extreme right, and I seem to be bent over the engine – as usual.*

39 — *Lady C in Hartington Grove after our return from Cornwall. The extended ammunition box contained our kitchen, and the wooden frame across the dickey seat carried a kitbag on each side. When raised, the hood afforded some protection to the passenger in the dickey seat, but that position was little coveted in inclement weather. As the driver, of course, I was exempt. We installed a telephone link, but there was too muchnoise for it to be of any use.*

Making money

Father was giving me 10/- a week pocket money at that stage; petrol was about 4/- a gallon, tyres were £3/15/-, inner tubes 15/9d, and so on, so I needed to supplement my income. I did this in a number of ways. First, I bred cactus and succulent plants in the lean-to greenhouse at the back of the house, and sold them at Miss Venner's greengrocery just up the road. Then I extended the greenhouse, and took over a business from Mr Stevens the school porter – breeding rats for dissection in the school biology labs (1/6 each).

Ray Woodman, a cabinetmaker, had just set up in business in a garage on the other side of The Lane, and I did some work for him at 1/6d per hour. He showed me a simple wooden puzzle which I then manufactured in great quantity to sell at school at 6d a time. The school was divided into two – those who had a puzzle and knew how it worked, and those who didn't and wanted to. Luckily, the first group was jealous of its knowledge and for a time I couldn't keep up with demand. Of course the demand was eventually satisfied, but I got a few gallons of petrol from the exercise.

At some stage I had the brilliant idea that there was something to be made – not a fortune, perhaps, but a steady income – from breaking Bentleys and selling the parts. Such an idea would be difficult to put into practice nowadays, but when there was far less regard for the historical significance of such vehicles it was possible to buy for a song a heap of bits that somebody with less time than he'd thought wanted to get rid of. Father would put up the money; I would do the work. We acquired quite a lot of material and advertised in *Motor Sport*. The flaw in the scheme soon became apparent. People wanted nothing but the 'D'-type gearbox and the 3.85:1 crownwheel and pinion. We had the laughable 'B'-type gearboxes, and the 4.32:1 crownwheels and pinions. (My data may be a bit ropy, but you get the idea.) With hindsight, of course, it was clear that we had a collection of durable items which – *ipso facto* – nobody wanted, and none of the expendable and much-sought-after components. We soon disposed of the collection as a job lot, and just about broke even.

John Stanford

In the year 1951, something happened which changed my life, though if it hadn't happened then I suppose it would have happened at some other time. The momentous happening was *seeing* jazz being played for the first time. Of course, I had heard it on the wireless and the gramophone, but that wasn't the same thing. I wanted to play jazz, but nobody knew how, so couldn't tell me. Then in the spring of 1951 I discovered that a jazz band played every week at the New Spring in Chesterton Road. It was Tony Short and his Sackdroppers, the first Cambridge University

Jazzband. They were Gods, and for the first time I not only heard the music live, but actually saw how it was done – that is to say, saw the mechanics of the various noisemakers that had hitherto existed merely as sounds. Heady stuff. The leader was, of course Tony Short, who played the piano – my instrument! The room was packed with people and smoke; you paid Brennan Jones, the treasurer, sixpence, and you were in. During the interval another pianist called Ieuan Lloyd Jones played boogie woogie, which elevated him to Olympus as well.

One bright Saturday afternoon soon after I'd passed my driving test I received a visit from the Gods – Tony Short and Brennan Jones accompanied by a newcomer, John Stanford who, as far as I remember, was not interested in jazz. At first, I couldn't believe they'd come to see *me* – indeed, seeing them out of context, I wasn't even sure that they were who I thought they were (but they were). It so happened that they'd come to talk about motor-cars because they were deeply interested in them (as were many discerning people in those days). They seemed as humbled to be offered a ride in the Rover as I was to receive them, so I guess we were emotionally quits.

40 — *On the first occasion I met Jones, Short (on the right) and Stanford we took a ride in Lady C. Here we are at Milton – as usual, I seem to be bent over the engine, and John is behind the camera.*

Tony Short (1923–1988) was a mature student at Magdalene, a 'renegade mathematician' as he described himself, reading modern languages. The mathematics helped to explain his interest in jazz; I later listed about 70 Cambridge jazzmen, almost all of whom were reading mathematics or sciences. Tony was a first-class pianist; I listened to him endlessly and learnt much from him. He later rejoined the RAF as an Education Officer; then switched services to the Royal Army Education Corps.

John Stanford (1929–1989), who was reading archaeology at Pembroke, had in turn a Clyno, a Humber, a Swift, and a Crossley before moving to what some would describe as the very epitome of Vintage Motoring, the 30/98 Vauxhall.

Here is his own account [1984] of those motoring days:

Vintage Motoring – John Stanford's Story

My first car was a Clyno which I was almost embarrassed to own. I tried a 12/25 Humber coupé, but it discarded its Dynastart chain before I realised what damage this could wreak inside the engine.

Then I dredged up an incredibly awful Swift Ten fabric saloon, and the relieved vendor also dumped upon me enormous amounts of Swift spares to make the bargain seem even better. Very serious parental resentment brewed as the garden filled month by month with Swift frames, gearboxes, cylinder blocks, and axle housings, none of which was the slightest use anyway, and which my own eventual victim sensibly refused. The Swift plodded on in a bovine way for quite a while, but I actually went to sleep at the wheel one hot July afternoon on a straight road near Norwich from sheer boredom, plus perhaps a suspicion of carbon monoxide in the frowsty interior. At Swift speeds this was no crisis.

41 — *A 10.8 Clyno at Bury St Edmunds, in dire need of a new set of boots. The 4-cylinder 66 x 100mm engine has a capacity of 1,368cc and develops 23bhp.*

42 — *The chain drives on the 15/40 Humber engine. 'In this example the exhaust valves are direct operated, and the inlet valves are of the overhead type operated by means of push rods and rocker arms. The method of compressing the valve spring for removal purposes is clearly shown in the illustration. It will also be observed that there are three separate silent chain drives, one from the engine to the camshaft with the usual two-to-one reduction, and a further drive from the camshaft to the lighting dynamo, shown attached to the crankcase. The left-hand chain drives the magneto.' The silence of the chains is shattered – as are more physical things – when something breaks, as John Stanford found to his cost when a newly-acquired Humber he was proudly driving home disintegrated at the Four Went Ways crossroads, near Linton.*

About this time [continues John's narrative] I became friendly, as did so many of his customers, with Cecil Bendall, whose emporium by the Railway station at Stevenage was a place of pilgrimage for all interested parties, always with a selection of extraordinary cars for sale at prices which do not now bear thinking about. Maybe he was perpetually hoping that I would bring him wealthy customers, but I didn't know any. Although disappointed in this, he was generous to a degree in loaning vintage cars for test purposes or proposing, often amid extreme hilarity, expeditions to far corners of England to buy or sell them. Even today, I can't pass through Kimbolton without thinking of the fine 8-litre Bentley which lay for so long unwanted at the back of Robinson's Garage; or drive through the Blackwall Tunnel without a picture of myself at the wheel of Richard Pilkington's 1924 4-litre Voisin, but at the end of a towbar, devoid of brakes, and riding on four D-shaped beaded edge tyres, following a rescue job in Bromley. I was later rewarded for this penance by several long drives in this exceptionally nice car, and there are many memorable motoring experiences for which I must belatedly thank CJB. These include some epic drives in his 1922 Silver Ghost, and a hectic evening at an RNAS station on the Solway Firth, where someone ate a wine glass.

43 — *John Stanford (right) at the Bwlchgwyn Trial, 1988, talking to Nigel Arnold-Forster and David Thirlby.*

———

The other pictures on these two pages were taken by John during our research outings.

44 — *A type 57 Bugatti Corsica which used to live at Rudd's Garage (as it was then) on the Huntingdon Road at Girton. According to John Stanford, it was a don's car, 'allegedly used by its owner for weekend visits to teashops with his wife. He was always very good about letting the interested have a look at this distinguished car but it was never seen on the road.'*

45 — *1925 14hp Bean in King's Parade. The car was somewhat heavy, even for its 2,385cc engine.*

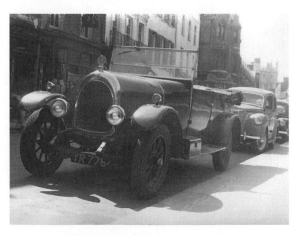

46 — a 12/25 Star taxi, well-known in Bury St Edmunds in the early 50s.

47 — Dr Roderick's 3-litre Sunbeam RF36. The 75 x 100mm engine develops 90bhp max, and the top speed was given as 'over 90mph'.

48 — A pretty Vauxhall 14/40 saloon which drove into our presence in Cecil Bendall's yard one afternoon. The rear-seat passenger looks less than interested.

Having determined to do better, I crept in the direction of the Bendall establishment with the remains of the Humber, plus yet another parental cash advance. Having owned nothing larger than 1600cc, I was surprised to find myself leaving Stevenage one dark night at the wheel of a 1923 19.6 Crossley of 3816cc. At last, a presentable car. Highly reliable, reasonably economical, and deliciously brakeless on its tiny little 820x120 tyres, it was excellent value for a somewhat steep £90, less £20 for the build-yourself-a-Humber kit. The Crossley served me very faithfully for several years, and in those happy and inefficient days one could write to Crossley Motors at Stockport and obtain minor hardware by return post, in linen bags. I was mortified to find, though, that the old thing had a residual value of only £42.17.6 by 1956; but by then I had my 30/98, and was on another motoring plane altogether – *VSCC Golden Jubilee Book 1984.*

49 — *John Stanford's 1927 Swift 10. The European Sewing Machine Company built Britain's first bone shakers in 1869. The following year it changed its name to the Coventry Machinists' Company and then built the very first high-wheeled 'Ordinary' (penny farthing) bicycle to James Starley's design. The Company began to build somewhat unconventional motor cars in 1902, and turned to cycle cars in 1913. After the war, they produced a 12hp and 10hp model, with the usual heavy four-cylinder side-valve engine with attached gear box. The 62.5 x 97mm engine of the 1190cc Swift 10 produced 22bhp and the car had a maximum speed of 50mph.*

Father, of course, had also discovered C J Bendall, and we often went over there to see what he had in his yard. Both Father and Bendall were great talkers, and used to amuse each other for hours while I wandered around the various vehicles soaking up the ambience.

Steve also went many times, and sat quietly in the back of whatever car it was, revelling in the rare marques and the motor talk.

She remembers particularly when we went to look at a car whose con-rod had broken and shot out through the crankcase. What happened when something broke in your engine? Did you slow down and come to a sedate stop, or was it like hitting a brick wall? We never found out.

At one stage I thought I'd like to restore an old car (*really* restore, that is, not take down clean and reassemble like the Rover). Needless to say, CJ had just the thing – a 1913 Phœnix. We couldn't go wrong at £17 (could we?); I think this included delivery, but I don't remember it arriving, just that it suddenly appeared in the garden, squeezed between the fence and the remnants of the privet hedge. We looked at the engine – seized solid. Usual approach – fill up the cylinders with Redex. Like the Henderson motorcycle, we revisited the Phœnix at ever-lengthening intervals but it never became free and at some stage Father got rid of the whole lot. I was rather glad, because it did need an awful lot of work and I had many other claims on my time (such as cactus growing, rat breeding, and schoolwork).

On one occasion CJ showed us a wonderful Edwardian charabanc with tiered wooden seating going up and up. It was tempting at less than £80, but even Father must have realised its impracticability – apart from anything else, it was too high at the back to fit in the garage. I don't remember that we ever bought anything from CJ apart from the Phœnix. He bought a car from Father many years later – to which we will come in due course.

Another place of pilgrimage was Conduit Head Road, where No 1 was a fine example of the 1930s architect-designed, white-painted, flat-roofed house of concrete-and-metal-window-frames genre. There lived an old Indian, H MacGregor Tampoe (Old Tampoe) and his son (Young Tampoe). We were first aware of their existence when we spotted their garden from the road; it was full of Bentleys, so Father drove in for a look. Out came the Tampoes to admire the $4^1/_2$, and we were taken on a tour of their extensive collection – not only Bentleys but other makes (Rolls-Royces, Daimlers, and one or two rarities such as the Arrol-Johnson).

Sometimes the Tampoes would arrive in one Bentley or another to see what we were up to this week; sometimes we would call on them for, even if there was nothing new in the garden, it was always a joy to revisit the old. I should record that the most memorable feature of all this for Father was 'Old Tampoe's hair' for it was silvery and very long but, instead of submitting to the force of gravity, 'curled up in great hooks at the back'.

When we weren't Bendalling or Tampoeing, John Stanford and I spent many a weekend driving round Suffolk looking for derelict cars in barns, hedgerows, *etc.* He was an inveterate taxonomist, and his tape measure clicked, and his camera whirred, as he collected details for the book he said he was going to write one day. In fact *The Vintage Motor Car*, by Cecil Clutton and John Stanford appeared in 1954, and ran and ran – and what a lovingly-researched work it is.

Alec Hodsdon

Le Papillon Bleu

One day, John and I went to Lavenham to see Alec Hodsdon, maker of keyboard instruments and owner of Veteran Cars. He received us cordially, and took us for a ride in his 1901 Panhard *Le Papillon Bleu*, which was exhilarating. The 1901 Panhard-Levassor had a 2-cylinder water-cooled engine, developing 7hp, a cone clutch, 3-speed sliding gear box, and side chain final drive. It had a rear entrance tonneau body and its price new in 1901 was £420.

Alec told us the story of *Le Papillon Bleu*. In 1901 Lesley Bucknall and J V Taylor had just sold a car and went to Paris in order to replace it. (Those were the days!) They could find nothing they wanted; moreover, no more would be available until the following spring. They went to the Panhard works and saw a beautiful car standing outside; it had been built to the very highest standards for a Director of the firm, the Chevalier René de Knyff. They were received by the Chevalier, who was reluctant to sell the car but said that if he *were* to sell it, it would have to be at an inflated price. How much Lesley Bucknall paid is not recorded but they struck the deal, and left the following morning. For some reason, Bucknall decided to proceed by train, leaving Taylor to bring the car home. 'I think he was realising that he had been foolish and was anxious to pave the way with Mrs Bucknall, who did not share his enthusiasm for cars, was apt to criticise what she regarded as his extravagance…' 'Twas ever thus.

The car arrived home, and was named *Le Papillon Bleu*. The brass plate we saw had been attached to it all those years ago while Vivienne, Lesley Bucknall's daughter, christened it with a 'bottle of the best, none of which was allowed to *touch the car!* '

On August Bank Holiday 1934, *Le Papillon Bleu* had the dubious distinction of being the first car to be damaged in the Mersey Tunnel, after its opening by King George V on 18 July. When Alec Hodsdon became the owner of the car, he sought out the Chevalier René de Knyff at his home in Paris. The Chevalier had written to him: 'Je suis content que ma vieille *Papillon* soit tombé en si bonnes mains et quelle faces encore de plaisir d'un sportsman'.

The 86-year-old Chevalier received Alec warmly, and went on to tell endless motoring stories, including one about the stranger who came to the Panhard works and asked for a demonstration run. There was no car available, but the visitor pointed to a car in the yard and asked why he couldn't go for a run in that. He was told that it belonged to a customer, who would doubtless give him a ride and who turned out to be none other than the Prince of Wales (later King Edward VII), while the customer was René de Knyff – the narrator – himself, before he became associated with the firm. The Prince drove him to his Hotel, but enjoyed the ride so much that he dismissed his equerry and went for a happy drive alone in the Bois de Bologne.

The weather was foul on the day of our ride, but all that is forgotten under the spell of going for a drive in an 1899 car with a fascinating history. We drove into Lavenham, and were immediately surrounded by admirers. Then we drove back and bedded *Papillon* down.

The Gardner-Serpollet

Next, Alec got out his 1904 Gardner-Serpollet Steamer, and lit the boiler. Nothing so smooth and silent as a steam car. What looks like a radiator is a condenser, and under the bonnet is a flat-four poppet-valve engine. The tin trunk at the back (**51**) houses the flash boiler. When it is running, the burning paraffin heats the pipes through which the paraffin itself flows, vaporising the incoming paraffin so that the flames continue to burn. To fire up, therefore, it is necessary to heat up the paraffin feed by external means, such as a gas poker or tray of burning methylated spirit.

50 — *The 1904 4-cylinder Gardner-Serpollet 'Tulip' steamer. Alec Hodsdon (right) has just thrown a match into the tray of petrol (whoosh!) which heats up the paraffin jets for the boiler – like a huge primus stove. The G-S has a flash boiler, similar in principle to an electric bathroom shower; the alternative way of raising steam is the pot boiler, as a steam locomotive has. The incredible 1904 hand-operated windscreen wiper is clearly visible. The car is on trade plates; her real number is CCV876.*

When steam is available, it may be admitted to the cylinders by moving a lever which controls not only the speed but also the direction of travel – showing the superiority of steam engine valve gear over the ICE gearbox. Another lever controls the donkey-engine which pumps water to the flash boiler, and the skill – or otherwise – of the driver is demonstrated by the ability to look ahead and ensure that the vehicle will take in its stride the undulations or other features of the approaching road rather than – literally – running out of steam.

Anyway, Alec fired it up, we all got in, and he drove it to a deserted airfield nearby. Would you like to try it? Would we! Even on our comparatively short journey we were able to experience the joys and woes of driving a steam car. I must say that we did very well, bearing in mind that, in addition to other duties, on that particular afternoon the driver had to manipulate the hand-operated windscreen wiper if he wished to have some view of where the car was going. It really gave us a feel for early motoring; after all these years the Gardner-Serpollet is still the oldest car I've driven.

51 — *The Gardner-Serpollet returning to its home after our dream trip on the airfield.*

I found driving any sort of old car most interesting – they all had their own peculiarities. Within a few months of gaining my driving licence I had driven 26 different cars, for I knew quite a lot of people who had sufficient faith in my abilities to let me have a go. One memorable vehicle was John Stanford's 1923 20hp Crossley ST2649 mentioned above. The 4-cylinder side-valve engine had a bore of 90mm and the comparatively long stroke of 150mm and, wrote John, 'it pulls a very high axle ratio (27mph being 1000rpm) resulting in surprising economy and ability to maintain its admittedly modest cruising speed of 45mph without the least appearance of effort.'

I remember that, during my spell in control, we were both momentarily shocked when I found for myself the inadequacy of the braking system mentioned above.

52 — In 1952, John Stanford, Robert Erskine (another archaeologist) and I went to Norwich for the day to seek out a number of cars on John's list. Here I am with Robert – (though I'm not sure which of us is which!) and the 1899 Panhard M22, a 2-cylinder 6hp phaeton, the property of Norwich Corporation Museums' Committee. As I recall, Robert's interest was more archaeological; he preferred vehicles which had to be dug out of burial mounds, and collected stories of cars which the owner had bought new in 1896, and which were burnt on a pyre at the funeral – good Grandfather's Clock stuff.

A GWK

On another of our trips we came across a rather rare GWK languishing in a garage with sunlight strobing in through chinks in the woodwork. Grice, Wood & Keiller of Maidenhead built a 2-cylinder friction-drive cycle car before the War; after the War (1923) they went for the ubiquitous 4-cylinder side-valve engine, but kept the friction drive. On the end of the propeller shaft was a friction disk a couple of feet or so in diameter, driving a wheel whose axis was at right angles to the prop shaft and parallel with the ground. The driven wheel could slide sideways on a splined shaft whose ends carried gears meshing with internal gear rings on the rear wheels. The speed of the car, forwards or backwards, depended on the point at which the driven disk pressed against the driving disk – how far from the centre, and on which side. The 'gear lever' controlled the lateral movement of the driven wheel but, although the gear quadrant was marked R-0-1-2-3-4, it was possible for the driver to select any point in the range – 'in fact,' says the instruction book, 'it will often be found advantageous only to change speed half-way from one notch to another.'

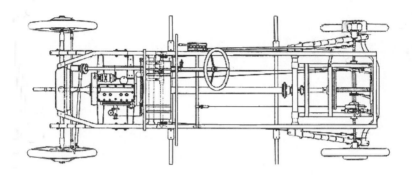

53 — *The chassis of the GWK. With its standard 4-cylinder side-valve engine it could maintain a speed of 37mph up hill and down dale all day and all night. The car had 4-wheel brakes, a transmission brake on the differential housing, and epicyclic-reduction steering.*

A further feature to assist starting, particularly on hills, was a heel-operated pedal to press the disks harder together; this avoided having to set the normal spring pressure too high. Some drivers complained that their gear always slipped, and that they could not discover the cause. It was suggested that such drivers 'are in the habit of keeping their foot on the clutch pedal while driving, and forgetting that the foot and a leg have a certain weight, and that they are in fact partly de-clutching.'

The whole system was simple and very elegant, but didn't catch on; perhaps drivers felt that if it didn't have meshing teeth, it couldn't really work. Nevertheless, in 1924 it was reported that the Maidenhead company 'boldly announce their intention of adhering to a system of drive against which much prejudice has been exercised but which undoubtedly has advantages over the normal gearbox' (*Light Car and Cycle Car* 5 September 1924). A fortnight later, the magazine was waxing lyrical on a test drive:

'To those who have never tried friction drive the transmission of the GWK could prove to be a revelation; its beauty is its very simplicity, particularly in control,

whilst the drive takes up a full load with all the firmness and tenacity of a clutch
. . . There is no hum or other unpleasant audible indication of the type of drive
fitted, whilst along gentle downward slopes one can coast with the discs apart,
the car then running with cat-like silence.'

I toyed with the idea of rescuing this car, but John dissuaded me; I
don't think he believed in friction drive either.

A Humberette

On another expedition, we came across a 1914 Humberette crumbling in
a barn at Long Melford. For some reason or other I became obsessed with
this car, and convinced myself that the owner would sell it to me for 50/-.
To shift it, I needed a trailer, which I didn't have, so I built one.

*54 — The 5hp single-cylinder Humberette first appeared at the beginning of the century.
The Humber Company then began to produce a large number of models, both at
Coventry and Beeston (Nottingham). By 1906, the range was reduced to two models. A
new factory was opened at Coventry in 1908, and the Beeston and Old Coventry works
were closed. The Humberette reappeared in 1913, with an 8hp air-cooled V-twin engine.
It weighed less than 7cwt so the RAC classed it as a cyclecar, but it was of sturdy
construction, with rack-and-pinion steering, three-speed gear box, $^1/_2$-elliptic springs at
the front and $^1/_4$-elliptic springs at the rear. The two-seater Humberette with hood,
screen, horn and lights, cost £125. The following year there was an alternative water-
cooled V-twin engine and according to the records, 2000 Humberettes were in use by
mid-1914. The one we found at Long Melford was one of them. See also (**4**).*

I took a spare Rover 8 frame, and bolted the front $^1/_4$-elliptics on back
to front. Then I attached a Rover front axle to these springs, but this had
to be back to front as well because of the arrangement of the holes in the
mounting plates. The back-to-front arrangement meant that the axle was

now more or less centrally-placed under the frame. Now I had to attach my new trailer to Lady C, so I took a brace and bit, drilled a hole through the floor under the dickey-seat, and suspended a chain through it – mindful of Harry Rooke's operation of 1945.

With the trailer fastened to the chain, I thought I was ready to go. The action of starting and stopping with the chain-means of attachment was rather exciting, and I began to understand why all other trailer drawbars in the world were rigid. But this problem paled into insignificance as I increased the speed of the test run up The Lane, and found the load becoming more and more of a drag until (as I saw in the mirror) the trailer wheels locked solid – odd, since it had no brakes. I soon diagnosed the problem; the front axle being reversed, the turning of the wheels tightened – and soon locked – their tapered roller bearings. In real life, these bearings had left- and right-hand threads in accordance with the axle being the way round that nature intended. I loosened the bearings and drove back down The Lane slowly, but I had to stop twice to free the wheels. I then admitted to myself that the idea that I might be able to buy the Humberette for 50/- was entirely my own, and that the recalcitrant trailer was merely proving that fact. It was clear from his relieved expression that John Stanford had never had any faith in the mission, and was glad that he hadn't had to take part in it – or even to veto it.

Thoughtful readers may wonder why I didn't attach the frame by its other end, thus restoring the orientation of the front axle. The answer is that the frame had no suitable cross member at that end, so it was just not possible.

Lorraine-Dietrich Silken Six – YP8563

Father unearthed a rare specimen of the 1926 Lorraine-Dietrich Silken Six – at Arrington, on the old A14. Hands up who's heard of the Lorraine-Dietrich. Since it actually worked (well, nearly) and the man wanted to sell it, Father went to negotiate and, after several visits, struck a deal. All we had to do now was to go and collect it.

By dint of being Sergeant i/c Signals in the school CCF, I had acquired a drum containing a mile of field telephone cable. I found the idea of owning *one whole mile* of cable very impressive, but the cable itself was very spiky and intractable, since it had six strands of steel wire (for strength) wound round a copper core wire (for conductivity), and a very tough outer sleeve. It could be severed (with difficulty) with a hacksaw (which lived up to its name) but the result was never very neat. Although I had also acquired a 10-line field telephone exchange, my visions of wiring our whole curtilage for telephonic communication soon faded, but now the cable came into its own. We plaited a rather laughable tow-rope from it, and set off with the $6^{1}/_{2}$-litre Bentley to collect the Lorraine-Dietrich.

All went well for some reason until we came to the home stretch, turning off Milton Road and into Hawthorn Way. It was there that the 'rope' gave out, leaving me gliding gently along in the middle of the road, wondering what to do for the best, while Father – whose knowledge of what was happening outside the vehicle he was driving was often wanting – disappeared into the distance. Luckily, we weren't too far from home, so he was soon back again. Heaven knows how long I would have had to have waited if I had become detached at the start of the journey.

The Silken Six was a very lively car; one of its main mechanical features was the row of exposed push-rods operating overhead valves. I used it quite a lot: it was a pleasure to drive and seemed to go very fast. At the time, I had no idea how fast it went because, like most cars we had, it had no speedometer – registered before 1937, you see. I now find that the maximum speed, according to the manufacturers, was 87mph.

55 — *Three-quarter nearside view of Lorraine-Dietrich outside our double garage in The Lane. The lower doors on the left are the stable, the taller ones on the right are the coach house.*

Of this car, John Stanford later wrote:

The silence of my parents' home was broken one summer day by a very refined sort of clattering noise, but I did not then know Leslie Winder's graphic comparison – 'ticks over like a weaving shed'. This certainly was apt, for the noise emanated from a 1926 20/60 Lorraine-Dietrich 'Silken Six' fabric saloon, which had somehow turned up in the Fens and been revived. It was a vehicle almost as ponderous as its title. We spent a happy afternoon driving the weighty arrangement and wondering how any derivative could possibly have run – let alone won – at Le Mans. Actually, apart from its Perpendicular appearance and quaint 3-speed gearbox the Lorraine was a pleasant old thing, and proved to be very practical and reliable.

56 — Lorraine-Dietrich engine, near side. It was a large car to have the petrol tank between the dashboard and the bulkhead.

57 — Lorraine-Dietrich engine, off side. The main feature to note is the method of operating the overhead valves by means of the long exposed push-rods.
The small raised oil-tank ensures that the valve gear is always well lubricated. Note the asbestos tape wound round the exhaust pipe. Father must have used miles of asbestos tape in his time.

Practical and reliable indeed – I used it quite a lot. One journey stands out in my mind: I took D Rintoul Booth, with whom I was at school at the time, to London to see a girl-friend (very daring). His sister Judith wanted to come with us; I was all for it, for our eyes had lately met across a clothes line, and it was *un coup de foudre* – love at first sight. The Booth family was off to Australia, so how was I to get to know this vision? Unfortunately, her mother wouldn't allow her to join us – for the uniquely motherly reason, I later found out, that her daughter might want to go to the loo. (It made no difference, Judith and I were married seven years later anyway.) So Rin and I were belting down the old A11 but, as we passed through Harlow, the car seemed to be going slower and slower. Eventually I cottoned on: it was seizing up. This was the first, but not the last, time this happened to me: one just sits and waits for the engine to cool and then fills up with water (and perhaps oil), drives on, and stops to inspect the levels at less and less frequent intervals as the memory dims until it happens again. This made us late but no matter. I can't remember what I did in north London until it was time to collect Rin, but when it became apparent that we were not going to get back until tomorrow, we set off at high speed. It was a filthy night, and in the middle of nowhere a yellow brick wall suddenly appeared in front of the bonnet, for the road had just sneakily turned left. Somehow, without losing speed, we got round the corner. Rin didn't say anything – I thought he was asleep, but he was actually in deep shock. I can conjure up that wall in my mind's eye as easy as anything.

58 — *The full-frontal Lorraine-Dietrich. Just visible are the transverse shock absorbers, the curious offset starting handle, and the top half of the Cross of Lorraine. 'Good pair of boots there, Dale boy,' Les Rich would have said.*

59 — *The 'Stork of Lorraine.'*

The Lorraine-Dietrich had a fabric body. Its end came when one of the undergraduate circle who had a moustache and therefore seemed more authoritative said that you could polish up fabric bodies like new with simple soap and water, and even offered to do it. Stupidly, we let him: the process removed all the waterproofing from the material, the roof began to leak, the frame began to rot, fungi appeared, and the moustachioed one disappeared – he sensed we weren't best pleased and was never seen again.

Father 'got rid' of the Lorraine – I can't remember whence – and it remains a fond memory triggered by its radiator mascot which Father always referred to as 'the Stork of Lorraine'. He had removed this for three reasons – it was dangerous, it was inviting to ne'er-do-wells, and he liked it and wanted to keep it. It was only when the buyer said: 'What a pity it doesn't have the stork mascot' that he realised it really *did* belong to the car. He had it in his raincoat pocket at the time, but didn't let on.

The Cluley 10.4 – DP5630

Another extraordinarily rare vehicle we acquired was DP5630, a Cluley 10.4; John Stanford was on the top of a bus to Ely, and spotted it on the back of a lorry at Jack Branch's yard in Waterbeach. JB wanted £25; Father offered £20. The deal was concluded by telephone; in a voice that could he heard all over the house, JB shouted: 'SPLITCHA' (he was on the *other* end of the 'phone, you understand) and the car changed hands at £22/10/- which was about 10% of its new price a quarter of a century before. What might it now fetch half a century later?

According to *The Motor* (25 March 1924) the Cluley was a small car with a fine top-gear performance designed to appeal as much to the novice as to the experienced motorist. 'Selling at £250, the 10.4hp Cluley two-seater makes, on account of its remarkable top-gear pulling capabilities, a vehicle which will hold a special appeal for those to whom gear changing appears a complicated and terrifying manoeuvre.'

60 — *Steve sits on the running board of the Cluley 10.4 as discovered on the back of a lorry in Jack Branch's yard at Waterbeach. Prominent features of the Cluley were the hub covers, which were extraordinarily protrusive and reminiscent of clowns' hats.*

The Cluley also had a Lucas Dynamotor; a combined starter and dynamo. The looks on bystanders' faces when a car suddenly bursts into life as the Dynamotor is energised are something to be remembered – and bear in mind that starting a car used to be rather more noisy than it is now. *The Motor* went on to say:

As a proof of the power of the Lucas Dynamotor, the car was driven a few yards by this means alone with the ignition switched off. This, of course, while making an excellent demonstration, puts a rather severe strain upon the batteries, and owner-drivers are strongly advised not to amuse themselves by propelling the car in this manner.

Our lawn was still covered with the barrage balloon on sticks, so the Cluley was moved into the Big Top and stripped down. The engine was seized, so we put Redex through the plug holes to try and save work. It didn't, so we removed the cylinder head, took a piece of apple wood (according to the experts it *had* to be apple wood), placed it on one of the up pistons, and thumped while pulling on the handle. It was disappointingly easy to free the engine, and within a few minutes it was reassembled and running smoothly and quite silently.

61 — *The front end of the Cluley chassis after reassembly, waiting for a test run. We have rigged up a temporary petrol tank and the all-important oil pressure gauge is attached to the steering column. The gearbox, with its great sloping top-plate, is quite large compared with the engine. A feature of the handbrake lever is its side ratchet.*

At this stage appeared a young naval officer, who was reading engineering at Cambridge, in an ambiguously-named group called 'U6'. David Brooke had heard of our Cluley and wanted to buy it. I was rather sad, because I had never got to know it, but we didn't really need so many cars, and he said I could have a go or three when it was reassembled. Furthermore, he and his friends undertook the reassembly, which was quite labour-saving – in some ways, but not in others. For instance, the rear axle was completely symmetrical, and the parts lay in fearful symmetry ready for reassembly. Have you guessed? They put it together with the crown-wheel on the wrong side of the pinion, and got one very slow forward speed and three increasingly faster in reverse.

We soon put that right and conducted extensive tests on the chassis as captured in the accompanying pictures.

62 — The complementary view of the Cluley about to emerge. The photograph shows a number of other (non-Cluley) features – the doors of our double garage opening on to The Lane, and the fact that Lady C has by now acquired a pair of shaped front wings, and running boards, the offside one of which is helping to supporting the spare wheel.

After all this, we popped the body back and were all ready for the open road. It was a Sunday afternoon, and David said that we were going round the Norfolk Broads – the only time, oddly, that I've ever visited them.

David, John Reeve and I took it in turns driving, sitting in the dickey seat, *etc*. It was on the outskirts of Wroxham that our hasty preparations came home to roost. A policeman stepped out (with his back to us) to usher a crocodile of children across the road. The brakes were not too good – rear wheels only, of course – and David pushed the pedal floorwards with all his might. The forces involved were such that the rim of the steering-wheel sprang off its spokes and the front seat, which had not been properly fastened, tipped over backwards. John Reeve, in the passenger's seat, had of course been pushing hard on the floor in sympathy with David, which made the fall much harder. Would the policeman turn round? The crocodile seemed thankfully endless as we clawed the seat upright again and tried to reassemble the steering wheel.

63 — *I don't think I'm towing the Cluley with Lady C, so exactly what is going on here is unclear – especially with John Reeve running along behind. This is at the de Freville Avenue end of The Lane*

64 — *David Brooke seated on the Cluley chassis during the tests observed by friends Andrew Beamish (left) and John Reeve.*

'Let's get out of here' was our only thought, and with great composure we were ready to drive away, as the kindly policeman looked over his shoulder, smiled rurally and waved us on. David had been unable thus far to spring the rim of the steering wheel back into position, so he steered by the spokes, supporting the detached rim plausibly on his wrists. We drove round a corner out of sight, parked, and dissolved into uncontrollable laughter as we put everything together properly. (David – see his recollections below – thinks it was a dog, not a policeman. It makes no difference to the events *inside* the car.)

65 — *David Brooke at speed on the autobahn. Clutton, Bird and Harding* (The Vintage Motor Car Pocketbook) *say of the Clyno: 'In the last year of its life there was a 9hp model which to the layman is virtually indistinguishable from the Cluley. As the authors confess themselves to be amongst those unable to make this fine distinction, the Cluley is not separately dealt with in this book.' However, the squarer radiator, and prominent drain-cock (see below – the fire-extinguisher system) give it away.*

Life with a Cluley – David Brooke's story

Wanting a car
Meccano was more fun than computers, and cars, before the production engineers got hold of them any way, were nice big mechanical toys, with the advantage that – sometimes – they provided a means of transport. All right, we expected to use public transport then, but that had its limitations, for example you couldn't sail at Cambridge unless you could get to St Ives, and there wasn't a bus. Not that I really wanted to sail at Cambridge as I couldn't be doing with the dinghy-racing mob, but I did miss my Meccano set.

I can't remember how I found Chesterton Road and the Dales. I think John Stanford was the lead, but how did I meet John Stanford? Anyway, one day I found myself there looking at two tea chests and a packing case and a body of sorts. Along with this went Rodney and his little sister, Mr Dale and his stable of motor cars (how big was it then? I'm not sure), Mrs Dale and Grandma. So apart from the mobile – sometime – Meccano set, there was this charming and welcoming family offering a home from home in the rather bleak, as I found it, College environment. These all-male places I had been dumped in since I was nine, and which looked like continuing, me being in the Navy, weren't very natural, and never really suited me.

Building it

The tea chests *etc* proved to contain a Cluley. What's a Cluley? Well, it looked like a Clyno, but wasn't. I never saw a Clyno, but they were reputed to be quite respectable cars, and their makers cannot possibly have known less about cars than Cluleys did. However it all went together pretty easily, and mechanically there didn't seem to be much wrong. I managed to find some ash to repair the bits of the body frame that were too dodgy. Several years later I was in a café of some kind when a kid rushed up to the next table saying 'Daddy – there's a car outside with our name on it!'. Apparently this was the very family, though a later generation, but they didn't want to talk about it – it didn't seem to be a part of family history they wished to remember. Of course the Cluley was less than 30 years old then, but just compare it with a 1968 car now! I think 90s cars are probably quite good on the whole, but it's probably as far from a Mk1 Vauxhall Victor to my 180,000 mile BM520 as it was from a Cluley to a half-timbered Morris. Further, probably.

The back axle

Two identical castings, non-floating half shafts, straight-cut crown wheel. It could be assembled in one of two ways . . . Now, which way does the engine go round? OK so *that* side of the pinion goes downwards, so the crown wheel goes *there*. Oh Rats! This car has three reverse gears and one forward. But that was only an hour's work to fix. I remember my mother telling me this was a common occurrence with Model T Fords.

The brakes

Or rather 'brakes'. Rear wheel only. Separate shoes for hand and foot brake. Rods about 18" long located in diff case at one end and back plate at the other. Drop arms half way along. Apply force to brake pedal. Result: rods rotate, brake shoes move apart and car commences to slow down. Apply more pressure, and the rods just bend in the middle, and the car doesn't slow down any faster.

Consequences

Somehow the front seat didn't get screwed down straight away, so on the first run when a dog crossed the road just ahead, very slowly, I tried to brake, with the result outlined above. Apply more pressure, and the seat gives way. Hang on to steering wheel and push harder. Steering wheel rim detaches itself from spokes. The dog was safely across the road by then though.

The clutch

Wet-cotton-faced cone clutch. This tended to slip, and finally got so bad that I failed to deliver a group of oarsmen to their regatta. This clutch really should not care about wear, so why was it slipping? Yet another dismantling finally showed up the problem. The clutch cone, having a narrow taper, moved a long way as things wore, and the very large bearing-cum-'oil-seal' at the front of the clutch shaft was hitting the bit ahead, preventing the cone biting. A 16-gauge aluminium cone was fitted inside the lining and the rivets replaced (with new ones I think, though this seemed rather a fancy thing to do), and it never slipped again for the many thousand miles it ran while I was associated with it.

The gearbox

Well-worn gears of the 'was involute' variety. What wasn't obvious was that the well-worn selectors could defeat the embryonic gate. So one day we were waiting at traffic lights in Beaconsfield. Lights change. Engage first gear. Release clutch. Nothing happens. Oh dear! The clutch has packed up completely. Select neutral, release clutch. Car leaps violently backwards. Fortunately, rear wheel brakes are quite effective in reverse. Leap out, remove floor boards, remove gear box lid, push reverse selector back, reassemble and proceed.

The fire extinguisher system

Wooden floor boards with gaps. Exhaust pipe with gaps in the flanges. This was quite useful at night as one could adjust the ignition timing until the flames went out. Also holes in the silencer, allowing hot gases to play on the floor boards. Result – 'Fire!' Leap out, remove floor boards, run round to front, hold boards under radiator drain (see **65**) until extinguished. Continue. (During assembly stage at Chesterton Road: RD: 'That's a nice drain tap'. DB: 'Looks a bit phallic to me'. RD: 'We should put a notice "Danger! Phallic Tap!" ')

The one-legged trouser system

Prop shaft has large fabric flexible couplings. Prop shaft balancing virtually impossible. I did get some new ones made eventually, which improved it a bit. Driving one day with the floor boards removed (Fire precautions?), left trouser leg gets tangled in flexible coupling. This could have been quite nasty. Years later when in hospital with TB after swimming in a dirty Dutch pond, I was in the next bed to someone who had done the same thing and was in hospital for weeks having his tendons reattached. Fortunately motoring expenses limited one's wardrobe, and the trousers were quite rotten, so the only problem was walking home in one legged trousers. Being Cambridge, no one noticed.

Magnetos

The magneto was low down on the near side, just where water shot up if one went through a puddle. This once resulted in my rushing into a pub with a magneto in my hand – 'Have you got an Aga please?' 'Yes we have.' 'Could I put this in your bottom oven for half an hour?' Nice people – they didn't bat an eyelid. They also sold some extra beer, I suppose. The mag was an 'ML' (?) 'Mushroom' magneto, which was past its prime. I started the usual lengthy trail for spares, but was in luck. All the college lawn mowers were of similar vintage to the Cluley, and there was a fitter somewhere in Cambridge who had all the magneto spares, distributor, points – even the shims needed for the old fashioned thrust races.

Tyres
700 x 85s were quite easy to get, but not really adequate. Eventually I found where to get 710 x 90s which transformed the car.

Pinking
It wasn't. It was big ends. Fixing these made an even bigger difference. Job done by Ted Salisbury in Cambridge.

Demise from my life
Driving to London one new year, with a nasty bout of flu brewing, and slow reactions. Sudden need to stop on the Great West Road near Osterley. Didn't make it, and went into the back of the car in front. This would normally have been unfortunate for the car in front, as the Cluley's dumb irons were prominent, to say the least, and would have made a nasty hole in most things. But it wasn't most things, it was a pointed tailed front drive Alvis, which stuck its tail through the Cluley's radiator. I left for Malta the next day, but my family managed to find a home for it while I was away. Incidentally, I went to an Alvis Register meeting in the Cluley once, and Patrick Campbell was there. The Cluley featured in *Lilliput* the next month as 'A sky blue car [it wasn't – it was Belco green] driven by a young man who resolutely refused to reveal his name'.

All in all the car caused infinite joy and infinite pain, but joy won.

The 8-litre Bentley – JVE820

As you will remember, Father had moved from a $4^1/_2$-litre Bentley to the $6^1/_2$ and now, fancying an 8, acquired GY7850. Well, in those days, the road tax was 25/- per horse-power (RAC rating) and the 8-litre was rated at 45.01hp, which made the annual tax £56/5/- or £15/9/5d per quarter.

This seemed a bit steep, but Father had a Plan. On 1 January 1951, the £10 tax was to come into force – for vehicles first registered on or after that date. If we scrapped GY7850 and re-registered it, it would be eligible for the £10 tax. The only thing was that the car had to be 'different', so how to achieve this? There was much discussion; changing the engine (a not uncommon act) did not – apparently – qualify for scrapping and re-registration, but changing the chassis did.

Father resorted to the old penknife argument: if you change the blade is it a 'different' knife? Both blades? The cladding on one side? Both sides? When does it become a 'new' knife?

Changing one of the cross-members in the chassis was the chosen route. There is a tubular cross member with a flange at each end riveted to the dumb-irons. Father drilled out the rivets, sawed through the tube, and removed the cross member. He then took it to Mackays and had a version fabricated with a central sleeve tapped with a left- and right-hand thread, and correspondingly threaded tubes with flanged ends fabricated to fit. The new member was placed in position and the central sleeve turned to screw the flanged ends apart to a snug fit. It was bolted into position – we had a 'new car'. Father then applied to register the vehicle as new.

66 — *The licence on the left shows the 45hp Bentley GY7850 costing £15/9/5d for its last quarter, and that on the right the car of private make using Bentley parts JVE820 costing £10 for the first year.*

When the men from the licensing authority came to inspect the vehicle, Father was out, and it was left to me to explain what we'd done.

'We've changed the chassis,' I said.

The men looked at the car, at one another, and at me.

'Well,' I went on, 'suppose we'd taken it all to pieces, and rebuilt it on a different chassis, would you say it was a "new" vehicle?'

They agreed that that would be classed 'new'.

'And suppose we'd rebuilt it, using some parts of the old chassis – that would still be classed as "new" according to your regulations?'

Again they agreed.

'What we've done' – I threw open the door to expose the open floor of the car – 'is to change this cross-member. As we understand the regulations, it must be classed as a "new" car.'

They agreed.

It was a memorable triumph, and the car was re-registered as JVE820. To celebrate, Father bought a road fund licence for a *whole year* – unheard of!

67 — The 8-litre Bentley engine. According to the records, the engine was 110 x 140mm, with a capacity of 7983cc, and the car had a speed range in top gear of 6 to 104 mph – 'unique'. The new chassis cost £1,850. The main problem, as I recall, was the Tecalemit Central Lubrication System. On the passenger side is a pedal which, when depressed, forces lubricant at 150 – 200psi into a system of tubes connected to key nipples on parts of the chassis. Do what one might, there were always some blocked nipples and some leaking ones – another good idea biting the dust. Father has sought to improve the appearance of the exhaust manifolds by painting them with a grey heat-resistant paint – but it soon started to flake off. Father's engines were never up to concours standard. I believe he took the view that it was a waste of time keeping an engine clean, and that a layer of grime helped to preserve it.

Father kept the 8-litre for a couple years, but I drove it only once, doing the ton on a deserted airfield. Ten years after he sold it, its then owner re-registered it as GY7850 and fitted a supercharger – I have yet to find out how fast it went then.

Before leaving the Bentleys, I will just mention that Father had one of the rare 4-litres for a week or two – unfortunately, I know no more than that about it. 50 were built from early 1931; the last was first registered in June 1933; two-thirds of them survive.

68 — *Re-registered, the 8-litre Bentley stands in Hawthorn Way. Directly behind it is our lovely lime tree and 142 Chesterton Road.*

69 — *Father's last 8-litre Bentley MMG329, which he owned between 1958 and 1962.*

The 1907 Darracq – DM270

Birch's Garage was in Victoria Road, presided over by Miss Birch and her brother-in-law Mr Howe. Old Mr Birch, founder of the business, had had a 1907 Darracq; it lived in the garage, and they had kept it in immaculate condition. This car was very similar to the well-known *Genevieve*, but three years younger.

The Darracq had a two-cylinder engine with the cranks at 180° so that it went chuff-chuff . . . chuff-chuff, but with a reasonably heavy flywheel it was hardly worse than half a four-cylinder engine.

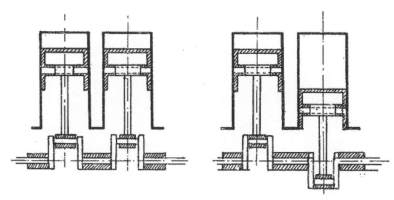

70 — *Two unsatisfactory arrangements for a two-cylinder engine. The first is equivalent to a single-cylinder engine (which is bad), but the power impulses occur at regular intervals (which is good). The second arrangement is better balanced than the first, but tends to impart a fore-and-aft rocking couple to the engine, and the power impulses are irregular – as on the two-cylinder Darracq*

Now, one of the events of 1952 took place in the Corn Exchange in Cambridge – an Exhibition for Accident Prevention Week.

How this came up I don't know, but Mr Howe thought that it would be rather fun to offer the Darracq to drive round Cambridge advertising the Exhibition. What was more, he invited me to take part, and who was I to disagree with him? He drove the car in the mornings wearing the false beard and top hat, and I was his 'lady' passenger (what a drag) as shown in the accompanying picture. In the afternoons I drove, wearing the false beard and top hat, with various little friends as lady passengers. It was a wonderful week, and I lost no sleep when I suddenly realised that I'd not had time to visit the exhibition!

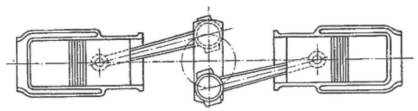

71 — *The arrangement of the two-cylinder horizontally opposed engine, as in the Rover 8: 'not only are the reciprocating forces very nearly in perfect balance, but the explosions occur at regular intervals.'*

72 — *Birch's Darracq travelling down Regent Street, Cambridge, about to pass the Regal Cinema. It must be morning, as I am the passenger, while Mr Howe drives.*

The Rolls-Royce Silver Ghost – SD6295

As the summer approached, 1952 became even more halcyon, for that year Father acquired his first Rolls-Royce – a Silver Ghost. The Silver Ghost was one of the longest-running models of all time, as it was built continuously from 1909 to 1925. He found SD6295 at Turner and Hore's garage in Newmarket – she had been a taxi but, having been built in 1919, she was deemed to be a bit antiquated so they thought they ought to get rid of her. Would – er – £50 be all right?

'That's a bit steep for a car built in 1919,' said Father.

'Well . . . it had had a new engine just before the war.'

'Oh, all right then.'

Thus we acquired a Rolls-Royce. The engine was still pretty good. There's a trick you can do if you have coil ignition and a manual advance–retard control: you switch on and flick the advance–retard lever and the contact-breaker will operate as the cap turns, sending a spark to the cylinder which contains compressed mixture ready to fire. And, as if by magic, the engine starts. It's very surprising – not to say impressive – to the onlookers and the quality of the pre-war engine was such that she could stand overnight without losing compression, and so 'start on the ignition' the following morning.

73 — *Father and the Silver Ghost in The Lane, 1952.*

SD was a beautiful motor; the chauffeur was supposed not to need protection from the weather, and sat in an open compartment, while the passengers were cocooned in the spacious room to the rear. For communication, there was a brass microphone with mahogany mountings for the passenger, and a speaker with a brown bakelite horn by the driver's right ear. The whole ethos is epitomised by the fact that (short of turning round and shouting) there was no means for the driver to communicate with the passengers.

I was privileged to drive SD many miles, and terribly glad to have had a father who not only had all these cars but encouraged me to 'take the wheel' as Ruth used to say.

One of the most memorable features of the Ghost was the governor, commonplace now, a revelation then. On the open road, one could set this control and relax in pleasure feeling it pulling up hills, easing back down hills, always trying to maintain the set road speed. I liked that.

When Father decided to get rid of SD, it proved uphill work to find a buyer (would that he had laid her up under dustsheets!) At last he found a film company who paid a grudging £140 for her to be disguised – they said – as an Hispano-Suiza in that baffling film with Humphrey Bogart and Robert Morley *Beat the Devil* (1953). Or so we always believed; for many years I was unable to take in the film because I was waiting for the appearance of the car, and after its filmic fall over the cliff I had little interest in the rest of the film. When I last saw it, I was able to concentrate rather better and came to the conclusion that the car featured was not, in fact, SD after all.

The Rolls-Royce Silver Ghost – NN3740

Our other Chesterton Road Ghost was NN3740, 1923 with added FWB, who came as a hearse.

'I'm not going out in that thing' said my mother (I expect), so Father bought a packet of blades for his hacksaw and a large tin of aluminium paint and proceeded to modify it; 'Dale's Sports Hearse' he used to call it. I'm sorry to say that I have no pictures of this car, as I had some rare old times in her – she stayed with us until the mid-1950s.

As befitted a large car, Henry Royce furnished his engines with both coil and magneto, each with its own set of plugs. So did WO Bentley, of course; since our earlier cars had been Bentleys, Father believed that *all* cars should have dual magneto/coil ignition, so the Silver Ghost was an acceptable model.

It was the coil that enabled you to perform the flick trick described above. If, however, the battery was flat, a sharp pull on the starting handle would have the same effect, because of the magneto. Now, one day NN's battery was flat, so I took it out and put it on charge. Later that day, I wanted to go out in her, so I started her on the handle to save the battery, and drove off. All seemed normal, save that the lights were a bit dim, but I thought that was hardly surprising. However, as I left the 30mph limit and increased speed into open country, the lights got brighter and brighter until suddenly they all failed simultaneously – pitch blackness, hold your breath, step on the anchors, and hope for the best. St Christopher was in full working order, I'm glad to say. Problem was, you see, that I'd forgotten to put the battery back again. Luckily, it was the fuse, not the lamps, that had blown so I adapted a piece of silver paper (the only good reason for smoking that I can now think of) and drove on with care and relief.

When I got home, I put the battery in so that I wouldn't forget. However, I left the pleasure of tightening the connectors until the following day, which was just as well because I forgot. There are two features of the Ghost with which you must be familiar for this account –

74 — *Off side of the Silver Ghost engine. Note (among other things) the cylinders in two blocks of three, the water pump, the distributor, and the wondrous carburettor.*

the first is that the battery lives in a box behind the front seat, the second is that the starter drives the engine via a sprocket on the front of the gearbox. It follows from the latter that, in order to start the engine, your gearbox should in neutral and your clutch engaged. Right.

Now, what happened was that in one of those moments of aberration I depressed the clutch, selected first gear, and pushed the starter button. The obvious result was that the car began to move forwards, the starter driving the road wheels via the gearbox.

Action 1	:	Release starter button PDQ.
Result	:	Nil; perhaps the contacts have welded.
Action 2	:	Make sure that the engine is switched off, and let in the clutch.
Result	:	The increased load slows down the forward movement, but the car doesn't stop.
Action 3	:	Try to change into neutral.
Result	:	Impossible, the load on the gear teeth is too great – nearly bend the lever.
Action 4	:	Perceive that the car is creeping inexorably towards the vehicle in front; try to steer out into the road to avoid it.
Result	:	Too close – too late.
Action 5	:	Dive over back of driver's seat and wrench the (fortunately untightened) leads from the battery.
Result	:	Car stops in the nick of time.

You see why it was a good thing that I hadn't tightened those connectors? This never happened to me again. Some time later, I was discussing the Night the Lamps Blew with Dave Rivett.

'You had the old Rolls that night, I seem to remember,' he mused.

'So did you, I seem to remember,' I riposted. Never forgotten.

The Ghost was quite thirsty. The handbook diffidently states: 'On dry, level roads, a gallon of petrol should carry a car of average weight with an average load at reasonable touring speed a distance of about 14 miles.' It gives no figures for stop–start town driving but when I went to work at Cathodeon, a distance of no more than three miles from home, I spent most of my £6 a week on petrol. It was totally fruitless, but tremendous fun.

Much is made of the story that the legendary Lord Berners had a grand piano in the back of his Rolls; in fact it turns out to have been a spinet – which is much more believable when you think about it. I bought a piano in 1955, which we collected in NN – no trouble. Father drove so that I could play it all the way home.

Father kept NN3740 for some years and, as with so many other of these interesting vehicles, I had the pleasure of driving her for many a mile. Ray Woodman – for whom I was working in the spring of 1955 – got the job of partitioning an office area for the new Magnetic Devices factory at Exning, near Newmarket. 8 x 4 sheets of hardboard and lengths of 2 x 2 were a bit much for his Austin 7 ('Mister E') and trailer, but Dale's Sports Hearse took it all in its stride and delivered team, tools and materials on site day after day.

Natural break

Soon, I was to go into the army for two years' National Service. I would not be returning to Chesterton Road, but none of us knew that yet.

As a lucrative leavening to the 'perishing books', Father used to earn 10/- an hour as a model at the Cambridge School of Art, where he was known as 'Dan' – for the alliteration presumably. He would turn up on his tricycle, or in the Sports Hearse (parking was easier then than it is now), and do his stint; he was a very good model since he could hold a pose for ages, and repeat it after a break.

He suffered a different sort of break in 1952, for he fell off the throne (that's what models model on) and was carted off to Addenbrooke's where they found he had a broken ankle and plastered him up. The first we heard of it was when he arrived home in a taxi and asked if I could go to the Art School and collect his tricycle. This I did, but I had not realised how distorted the tricycle was. Years of riding on cambered roads had gradually bent the front forks out of alignment so, in addition to the difficulties in steering this particular model, I'd just about got the measure of it when I arrived home.

There was more. Those used to starting a car on the handle know about keeping the thumb out of the way in case it backfires, and after several years at it my safety grip was automatic. It didn't, however save me from a Lady C backfire and a Colles' fracture (what little old ladies get when they slip on the wrong sort of leaves). So it was my turn to go to Addenbrooke's and get strapped up.

Shortly after that we were having difficulty starting some vehicle or other, and there we were in Chesterton Road, Father pushing, hopping along like some great spider with a crutch with his leg in plaster and me keeping my right arm well out of the way – a strange sight, unfortunately not captured by the camera.

Part 3 : NATIONAL SERVICE 1953–1955

Basic training

My first intensive phase of vintage motoring came to an end on 19 February 1953 when, having cashed the (uncrossed) Postal Order representing the Queen's Shilling, I arrived at Gibraltar Barracks, Bury St Edmunds, in a Bentley driven by Father. For a few seconds – while I disembarked and said goodbye outside the entrance – I commanded some reverence, but it quickly evaporated when I explained my mission.

This was the beginning of six weeks' square bashing with the Suffolk Regiment, and a military band playing *Speed the Plough* still frissons my spine. A lot happened in those six weeks. At the start, I wasn't allowed a car, but a letter to the CO soon cured that. However, before I nipped home to collect Lady C, the family came to see me and took me out to tea – I must by that time have learned to work the system to secure a temporary pass.

75 — *A promotional shot of a Speed Six that Father didn't buy some time in the early 50s. It is very similar to the car in which the family travelled to see me at Bury St Edmunds. UV1928 is very much alive today.*

They arrived in, I think, a Speed Six that Father had for a short time, and we drove back along the road to Cambridge until we came to the Greasy Caff, next door to an oil drummy sort of garage reminiscent of

Old Thoday's Place. This was fortunate, because steam appeared to be coming from under the bonnet, which drew out the garagiste – a Mr Mulholla – an Indian who had been a member of the Le Mans Bentley support team and therefore knew all about them – he said.

The problem was diagnosed as a hole in the elbow that bolted on to the radiator header tank and to which a hose was attached with a jubilee clip. Mr M first tried Radweld – a vain gesture in view of the size of the leak, but he had to try, I suppose, and at least he could charge 1/6 for it. The other cure for a leak in the water system – breaking eggs into the radiator – was presumably rejected as being too amateur, or perhaps there was a shortage of eggs.

His next line of attack was to remove the hose and the elbow, so that he could solder on a patch, he enthused. I knew this was going to be difficult because it was plain (at least to me, but obviously not to him) that the elbow was of a diecast aluminium alloy which spelt trouble. And so it was – he spent a long time cutting and shaping a patch, but when he applied his soldering iron to the casting it just disappeared.

That was one of the shortcomings of that alloy material – I had already experienced it when I endeavoured to mend a dashboard switch unit whose frame was made of it. Even Father began to get agitated when Mr M pretended that nothing had happened and decided to fasten the patch with 'some special tape we used to use in the pits'. To us it looked like insulating tape.

Meanwhile Ma and Steve were eating disconsolate egg sandwiches in the Caff next door. At last we were able to join them but I had very little to say – my purpose had been to get away from the barracks, and it seemed to me that to try to explain my daily life to people who really couldn't visualise what I was on about was a non-starter. Eventually it got dark, Father ran me back to Gibraltar Barracks, and later reported that he had driven home topping up the radiator every few minutes. He soon bought a new elbow made of a superior material, and all was well.

Gibraltar Barracks

Life at Gibraltar Barracks wasn't soft, but it wasn't meant to be. It was a little more bearable because a friend of mine from school was already there – he was what one of the Sergeants was wont to call a 'portential officer'. Gibraltar Barracks looks more like a castle, or a prison; the barrack blocks were named after 18th-century battles in which the Suffolks had excelled, and lacked every modern convenience.

Each recruit had a bedframe, and a locker made of hardboard. There were about 60 people in the intake, 30 of them in my barrack room. Cpl Fox, as low and cunning as his name, presided over us. The Army was full of Cpl Foxes, and it is difficult to imagine them existing anywhere other than where they were. The information content of his speech was severely impaired by the interspersed imprecations, which made it difficult to retain the thread of what he was saying.

In some semblance of order, we were marched to the bedding store to draw our bedding. We were shown how to present it 'boxed' – folded in the regulation way – and at once began to devise methods of making the task quite painless, such as 'acquiring' a duplicate set of bedding for nocturnal use and keeping an inspection set neatly folded and boxed for ceremonial use. We were marched to the clothing store – which was in the crenellated tower you can see from the road – and issued with the appropriate quantities of this and that. The most impressive feature of this exercise was the CQMS, who looked at each of us in turn and rapped out '15, $15^{1}/_{2}$, $14^{1}/_{2}$, 16, 15 . . .' and so on, whereupon a minion would issue the appropriate shirts which, astoundingly, always seemed to fit. This activity seemed doubly clever to me, for I had never before realised that I had a collar-size. We later discovered that most of the guesses were wrong, but nobody dared to complain.

Those weeks were a flurry of getting up at 05.30 hrs, washing in cold water, going on parade, doing PT, 10-mile route marches in full kit, being taught about rifles and Bren guns and field formations and camouflage and all the things that a soldier needs to know.

I said washing in cold water, but some of us discovered – a closely guarded secret which we kept – that the portential officers had an ablutions with hot water as well, and some of us took to going there (illegally) for obvious reasons.

The activities were punctuated with enormous meals washed down with limitless tea in our pint mugs, cookhouse fatigues, and guard duties. There was not, of course, supposed to be anything particularly pleasant about cookhouse fatigues, but once one had learned to cope with live steam and boiling water coming out of unlikely spouts at random, it was really quite easy and all repaid by the unending supplies of crispy bacon, fried eggs, fried bread, sausages, and tomatoes – a 24-hour breakfast laid on by the Army Catering Corps all over the British Empire.

In those days National Service was a 2-year term. It was noised abroad – and I suspect this was a rumour started by the regular Army afresh for each intake – that those who signed on for the minimum regular term of three years would *not* be sent to Cyprus, then a current trouble-spot. I thought then that those who fell for this did so because they thought it would make Army life easier for them. I think now that the Army life was far superior to anything they had experienced before, and they were only too happy to secure it for a longer time.

There is no doubt that those of us who had led sheltered lives up to that point – which was all of us, whatever the condition of our shelter – learnt a tremendous amount from being thrown together with a remarkable cross-section of humanity. Even those whose outlooks had supposedly been broadened by boarding schools found that there was still a very long way to go in learning how to live with their fellows from other walks of life, one of the great benefits of National Service.

Guard duties lasted multiples of twelve hours with three pairs of you on duty for two hours and sleeping fitfully for four. Seven people would go on parade, the odd one being 'stick man' – the best-turned-out of the bunch who was allowed to fall out and escape the guard duty. This of course was a transparent way of getting everyone to look as smart as possible, but for some reason I was always (with one exception) stick man. Could I, on whose report a school teacher had once written: 'Tries to excel without effort' be so smart so consistently? Perhaps the answer lay in the twin facts of my possessing a car and our being confined to barracks in the spring of 1953 because of the danger of East Anglian floods, which we were notionally prepared to repel at any time. The permanent guard corporal had a girlfriend in the town, and when I was stick man he would immediately seek my co-operation in driving him down to see the wench. As some sort of palliative he would bring me a large helping of fish and chips from the shop in which she served.

Wilton Park

Intake 53-04 (the fourth fortnightly intake of 1953) divided into four groups. There were a few who could not read or write – another salutary discovery – who were taken off for an intensive course in those arts. There were those who were going to remain as infantrymen in the Suffolk Regiment. There were the portential officers, who were on their way to Eaton Hall for the dreaded WOSB (pronounced 'wosby' – War Office Selection Board). And there were a few, like me, who were going off into some specialist trade, in my case the Royal Army Education Corps.

After six weeks, when the change – as seen in old propaganda films – from a shambling, gangling collection of individuals to a coherent body of quintessential smartness had been wrought, we had a passing-out parade and I loaded my few belongings into Lady C and drove from Bury St Edmunds, via Cambridge, to Wilton Park at Beaconsfield, the HQ of the RAEC. In ten weeks, those of us who survived the course (all except two of my intake) would be transformed into Sergeant Instructors. That meant that we had not only to learn all about methods of instruction (which in the Army are not basically different from those anywhere else, just more intensively and effectively taught) but also how to be Sergeants – able to take parades and hold our own Sergeants' Messes peopled by hardened regulars many of whom had experienced some war service.

The cultural atmosphere at Beaconsfield was several orders of magnitude more elevated than that at Bury St Edmunds. Even the camp hairdresser (in more ways than one) was an ex-Paratroop Captain, the walls of whose salon were covered with his insignia, medals, photographs of him standing by aeroplanes, rolling about on the ground with a parachute streaming out behind him and so on.

Drill practice on the parade ground, when each of us took turns in commanding the others, took on a new dimension, when the profanities of our basic training units were exchanged for such adventurous orders as: 'As you were – let's have it homogeneous this time' and: 'Get fell in properly, no more bloody parallelograms.'

The CO, Major Joe Waters, remonstrated with us – perhaps he had been nobbled by the Paratroop Captain – 'Gentlemen, it appears that you have been cutting one another's hair. I don't like it. It looks like a charade for the 39 steps.'

Captain Bill Sallabank was a man whom we all liked immensely. He seemed rather out of place in the army; for example, he failed to notice when inspecting the parade one day that I had my belt on upside down – and with blanco-covered brasses. Or perhaps he just didn't like to say anything. He was orderly officer when I found a jagged piece of tin in my pilchards. He bore it away to the kitchen, returning a long time later with the immortal finding: 'They say it shouldn't have been there'.

The course ended with Teaching Practices. Using the techniques we had learnt, we had to give a talk on a subject of our choice, on which our future in the RAEC would stand or fall. Father having exposed me to their wonders from an early age, I chose to talk about locks and keys. I spent hours making elaborate visual aids and – what I thought would be peculiarly impressive – constructing a large pair of compasses for drawing chalk circles on the blackboard. The difficult part was working their use into my talk.

Joe Waters had a list of all the TPs, and would drop in on those which he thought he might find interesting. My presentation, if I say so myself, was brilliant – the only thing I hadn't considered was tailoring the length of my talk to the time available. Thus it ran, with the blessing of the staff, over three periods – but everyone seemed to find it enthralling. I was invited to the Officers' Mess in Wilton House, not for some fantasy award such as an instant commission for my prowess, but to see if I could open the built-in safe in the hall. I demonstrated the principles on which the safe *could* be opened to an admiring crowd of officers, but lacking the necessary equipment was not then able to practise what I preached. I explained what I needed, and offered to go away and get the necessary implements, but fortunately my putative skills were not put to the test, and the safe remained firmly closed.

We were all granted 18-hour passes for the Coronation on 2 June. That meant that I could leave the camp at 0600 hours, and I climbed into Lady C and drove home. The journey took about three hours, as it always did, and I spent the day dozing in an armchair with Richard Dimbleby's wireless commentary washing over me. In the evening, I climbed back into Lady C and returned to Beaconsfield by the statutory 23.59hrs. That was my Coronation.

As the end of our course approached and we knew who had passed and who was, as they say, RTU, the next announcement for which we waited in trepidation was our posting. I found that I was to go to the Education Centre at Shorncliffe Camp on the south coast between Hythe and Folkestone. I loaded rather more belongings this time into Lady C and drove, via the Blackwall Tunnel, into Kent.

Shorncliffe

Shorncliffe Camp lies on a plateau above Sandgate and on a clear day you can see features on the French landscape with the naked eye. It was built before the Napoleonic Wars, and it was here that Sir John Moore of Corunna fame trained the famous Light Brigade. The camp, round three sides of a square, was built to accommodate more than 5,000 troops and, in 1897, a convalescent home with accommodation for 230 patients was built halfway up the hill between Sandgate and Shorncliffe. This was the home of No 10 Company and Military Hospital, RAMC, to which I was soon attached. Before that, however, I spent a little time in the Education Centre at the top of Hospital Hill.

The most memorable character there was WOII 'Waxy' Wilson. Waxy had been in the army for what seemed an incredible 25 years, starting in the cavalry which is where he got his nickname. How he got into the RAEC was a mystery to all of us, for he was no great intellect and spoke, for example, of 'a face by Vincent', meaning 'a portrait by Van Gogh'. Nevertheless, to us young Sergeant Instructors, suddenly plunged into whatever realities Army life held, Waxy was a benign father-figure who did much to make life bearable when we felt low.

In due course I was posted halfway down the hill to the Military Hospital, with the brief of providing education to the medical orderlies, and looking after and issuing the occupational therapy supplies, which turned out to be racks and racks of rug wool of all imaginable colours, and balls of string for 'Weaving, Netting and Knotting' – arts which, I'm glad to say, I was never called upon to teach. However, the patients were never there long enough to take up any occupational therapy, so most of my time was devoted to trying to set up classes for the medical orderlies. Unfortunately, the CO was not particularly keen on education, and had a habit of arranging (I thought deliberately) duty rosters to clash with my education rosters.

I made little use of my training for ten months. There was, however, plenty going on. At the beginning of my stay at Shorncliffe, I lived in a barrack room on the Sir John Moore Plain, and ate in the Sergeants' Mess up there. Later on, the Military Hospital acquired its own Sergeants' Mess, which was much more cosy, and in which I lived. This meant that I was able to move in all my recording equipment, which comprised record player, tape recorder, disc-cutter, amplifiers and so on, and I spent much of my time producing sound effects for the Christmas play.

76 — *Lady C outside the Military Hospital Sergeants' Mess at Shorncliffe.*

Rosemary Vickery was the St John lady who looked after the library and welfare in the hospital, one of the few women on the camp – apart from Matron who was a QARANC, and therefore untouchable. Rosemary loved Lady C and had a wicked sense of humour and we went out together quite a lot, though she always made great play of the fact that she had the status of lieutenant and should not, strictly speaking, hobnob with other ranks. We went to see *Genevieve* at Hythe and thereafter were intoxicated with the exuberance of our velocity – and verbosity. Eventually, she was posted to Kobe, whence her replacement came. Her parting jape was to tell me, in confidence, that the incoming girl was very sensitive about her name which, Rosemary whispered, was Ermyntrude. I have always wondered what she told 'Ermyntrude' my name was.

For a time, the Mess was overseen by a somewhat coarse WOI, whose habit of licking the stew off his knife before taking butter was offset by his ability to quote endlessly from the plays of Shakespeare in a fluent but quite monotonous voice. This was apparently the only advantage of having been incarcerated in a Japanese prisoner-of-war camp.

I slept opposite one of the new National Service Sergeants in the RAMC. He was as tall and thin as a hop-pole and an overt Christian, spending long periods kneeling by his bed. I had a love–hate relationship with him, in that I found it impossible to reconcile his thorough niceness with the almost macabre fact that he was engaged to marry a twelve-year-old girl whose family thought that it was marvellous, because of his Christian calling. I developed an intense desire to take hold of his bed and flip it upside-down with him in it, a feat of strength which I was convinced I could perform. It was nothing like as easy as that and, quite cleverly, he thanked me profusely and suggested that I should take a long-overdue bath. So I went into the bathroom, not noticing until later that the bath-plug had no string on it (this was fortuitous, not malicious). So there I was, kneeling in rapidly cooling dirty water, trying to saw up the plug with a razor blade which broke into ever smaller pieces.

My chief on-duty haven was the dispensary. Here was available any pharmaceutical chemical, and the speciality of the Sergeant dispensers was a range of delicious liqueurs based on an endless supply of absolute alcohol. The basis of any racket, I believe, is to run it so modestly that there is no reason why you should ever be found out, and they never were.

I was not sorry when the time came for a posting, for I was not really doing the job I had been trained to do. However, I was somewhat taken aback when I was offered a posting to the Far East, and intimated that I was not very keen on the idea. I don't lose very much sleep over that piece of foolishness, but I do feel from time to time I ought to have been a little more adventurous. I packed up and Father came down in NN to help transport all the stuff I'd collected. (He too was impressed with the knife-licking Shakespearean.) I trundled home for a week's leave and then, in May 1954, set out for Hamburg.

BAOR 12

I took a train to Parkeston Quay, where, it seemed, all the British Army had congregated. How was anybody to know who we were, or where we were going? We found ourselves in a Nissen hut which seemed to be several miles long, made dimmer by a 15-watt bulb every hundred yards or so, and shuffled through slowly, giving pieces of information; gathering pieces of documentation, until at last each of us was assigned to a particular journey – in my case to Hamburg.

Those of us who were ready to embark moved slowly forwards, carrying our kitbags and cases, and eventually found ourselves in an enormous space in the bowels of a troopship filled with bunks in three tiers. I laid claim to a top bunk because I thought, erroneously, that the air would be clearer up there. Nevertheless, having mastered the art of undressing sitting on a net with a metal ceiling covered in naked pipes about two feet above me, I got some sort of night's rest, developing a technique for breathing in when the boat went down and out when it went up (or perhaps the other way round) to allay any feelings of queasiness.

The following morning, the boat had arrived at the Hook of Holland and we found ourselves in another Nissen hut where breakfasts were served. There were military trains bound for destinations all over Europe, whose routes were distinguished by colours. Mine, to Hamburg, was the Red Train and our next step – or rather hop – was from one sleeper to another down a railway track in the middle of a marshalling yard, until we reached an embarkation platform. (I read recently that the goose-step was devised for marching along railway sleepers.)

We learnt a very peculiar thing from those returning – that on the way out we would think that the food was delicious, and on the way back we would think that the same food was terrible. This, we were told, was because the food in German messes was so good. On the train we ate succulent sausage, and potatoes fried in several different ways, and it was delicious.

The most memorable part of the train journey was passing through the bulb-fields of Holland. The train stopped at Utrecht, owing to the fact that the lines went no further. However, they put an engine on the other end of it and pulled it out in a different direction, and eventually we arrived in Hamburg. Of all the people who were going everywhere, three of us were education sergeants destined to be dispersed over the face of Germany. We arrived at a sergeants' mess very late that night and decided to put to the test our newly-acquired knowledge that alcoholic beverages were very cheap.

'Vot vould you like, gentlemen?' asked the German barman in not unreasonable English.

'Dry Martini', I said, feeling rather grown-up at getting in first.

'Certainly', replied Fritz (that was his name), busying himself behind the bar. He turned round with three glasses of Martini.

'That'll be 9d.' It seemed cheap enough, so we had a good laugh at a lesson learned, and drank up. We were brought a snack comprising mainly succulent sausage, and potatoes fried in several other different ways, and were not sorry to go to bed.

We spent a fortnight mostly sleeping, and learning how to live in BAOR, including the mysteries of BAFSVs – pronounced 'baffs' meaning British Armed Forces Service Vouchers – paper money which came in all denominations from one halfpenny to £1.

I was entrained to Münster-im-Westphalen, where I was to be attached to No 1 Wireless Regiment BAOR 12. Our barracks had been built by Hitler during the 1930s, and were of the highest standard of construction. I was introduced to the marvels of central heating, double glazing and snooker by my new colleague Schoolie Porter, whose successor I was to be.

Education guardian

I learnt that the CO was very keen on education – which made a change – and that the routine was that every month we would teach English, maths and current affairs to a class of about 20 men, at the end of which they would sit – and pass – their Army Certificate of Education (Third Class). Every three months, we would run an ACE Second Class course. Lastly, we might be roped in to teach those who were taking ACE First Class – which was said to be about O-level standard – at the local HEC (Higher Education Centre).

The staff at No 1 Wireless Regiment was drawn largely from the Royal Signals and the Intelligence Corps. The teaching staff – now two RAEC sergeants – was augmented by an instructor drawn from the Royal Signals, Donald Ingleton, a splendid chap and the only person from that period of my life with whom I'm still in touch.

I never felt passionately enough about current affairs to want to teach them so I left that to Don and Schoolie Porter, concentrating on what was called maths but was, in fact, simple arithmetic. We set our own exams, working to a pattern to maintain the standard. In the English paper, one of the obligatory questions was always a comprehension test, based on a newspaper report. We were avid consumers of suitable paragraphs of the 'Garden Shed Blaze' variety for use in class, and we saved particularly choice ones to set in our exam papers. One month, we were completely unable to find a suitable paragraph so we wrote our own, ascribing it to a fictitious publication called *Orb and Sceptre*. How gratifying to think that a copy of this examination paper is somewhere enshrined in the BAOR archives. *Caveat lector.*

While I was there, about 160 people must have passed through our hands; only one of them failed, and he passed on the retake. I concentrated on maths and map reading for the Second Class courses, which did at least give us a chance to get out into the countryside and try and find out where we were. I was invited to teach the one candidate for First Class physics, which I supposed I could do, since I had passed Higher Certificate physics myself within living memory. However, having prepared a teaching plan for this one candidate I was never put to the test because he was then posted out of reach.

Following the results of the ACE First Class it was customary for the examiners to send round a booklet assessing the examination. One particular comment delighted me, in the section on the English paper where, in one question, candidates had been asked to comment on John Masefield's poem *Cargoes* – which of course contrasts craft and their cargoes in time and space. 'Quinquereme of Nineveh from distant Ophir' is the opening of the first stanza and 'Dirty British coaster with a salt-caked smoke stack' the opening of the last. And, according to the assessment, one candidate had written indignantly: 'It's all very well for

Quinqueremes, sitting in their palaces at Nineveh, to criticise our shipping for being dirty, but they haven't been through a war like we have.'

The hidden curriculum

The work was good, sound, solid, stolid stuff which occupied us during working hours. Outside working hours there were various activities in which one could partake but I tended – stupidly, I see with hindsight – to avoid them. What an opportunity lost to learn to speak German. However, I discovered – and I know not how this came up – that if I were to pass an Army driving test I could then teach other people to drive and their army licences would be valid in civvy street. How could I get an army driving licence? It was very easy. Sgt Adcock (RASC) drove me out into the country in a fast little army vehicle of forgotten make and asked me to drive back again. I did this and was pronounced fit to teach others. I was given a truck of my own – 72RF31 – looking after its maintenance and preparing it for its 406 inspection every month just like a real Driver; no concessions to a Schoolie.

77 — My 3-ton Bedford 4 x 4 QL – 72RF31. Schoolie Porter (left) was one of my first pupils, but was demobbed and off to agricultural college before taking a driving test.

Three of my pupils will remember my driving instruction. The first was WOII Ferguson who, although he was in the Intelligence Corps, was unable to negotiate corners fluently. We would drive along one side of the perimeter road of the barrack square in fine style until we came to a corner. Then he would have to stop and inch round very gently; he could never drive fast unless in a straight line. Eventually he admitted defeat and gave up.

The second problem pupil was Lieutenant Andrews. We went out one dark and rainy night – I can't think why, for many of the roads were cobbled and were pretty dangerous at the best of times. This was the worst of times, and Lt Andrews got cold feet and asked me to drive back. Unfortunately, I myself ran into difficulties on the wet cobbles and completed the last waltz with a civilian Volkswagen embedded in the chassis. There was an official enquiry, and I received an official reprimand, but the Volkswagen driver was unhurt and they didn't take my truck away from me.

78 — *72RF31 in reverse*

My third client, who perhaps remembers me for a more laudable reason, was John Elmer, with whom I had been at school and who was now a signalman, the only person who actually passed his army driving test as a result of my efforts.

Another way of passing time was to take a turn on the telephone exchange. There were two PMBX positions, where two signalmen knitted pianos 24 hours a day, another skill which I thought it would be worth acquiring. However, the WO at the HEC was at first understandably puzzled, then incredibly angry, to find me answering the phone from the switchboard when he rang up. He put paid to that activity – except at hours when I knew he wouldn't be calling. During the quiet hours of the night we would have competitions ringing from exchange to exchange round the BAOR network, to see who could get through to the other first.

Character set

At Münster I shared a bedroom in the sergeants' mess with three others, one of whom, Sergeant Platt, was a stickler for rules and probably didn't like National Service sergeants very much anyway. His chance came one morning when I was late on parade – we used to take it in turns running the parades – and he put me on a charge. We marched into the CO in double time just as you see on the films: I not wearing a beret to show that I was the prisoner. The CO looked very puzzled. Sergeant Platt explained what had happened in a monotonous, megaphone voice. The CO still looked puzzled. At last he spoke: 'Sergeant Dale, make sure you get up on time in future. Sergeant Platt, don't be so bloody silly. Dismiss.'

Having had to save one of my other room-mates from choking on his own vomit, I decided to claim a one-man room for my own, and for the rest of my time in that Mess I went to bed early most nights with a good book, a pint of orange juice, and a box of Crunchie bars.

Hearing that I was interested in tape-recording, the WOII at the local HEC wanted to show me his. It was an enormous Grundig machine seemingly covered in magic eyes, which, he said, had cost him DM10,000. Suddenly, he commanded me to sit at a piano and play something for him to record. It was at this point that it began to dawn on me that he was not quite sober and when he began to dance and clap his hands my suspicions were confirmed. Suddenly, he collapsed into an armchair and asked me: 'How are you getting on with Sergeant Porter?' Without giving me time to answer – if indeed there was an answer – he went on: 'Sergeant Porter is a real son of the soil. He's the salt of the earth is Sergeant Porter.' I could see his eyes brimming with tears. 'Sergeant Porter is the salt of the soil – a real son of the earth . . .' and so it went on. When he started to snore, I left the room and returned to No 1 Wireless Regiment. I never saw him again – apparently there was some mystery about the way in which he had acquired his expensive tape recorder, and he was removed from his post, BAOR, *etc*.

As time went on, and I became more confident of wandering out into the streets of Münster, I found that there was a rather good Toc H bookshop, where I purchased several of my still-favourite books. The walls were adorned with pictures of traction engines in steam and, finding that I was interested in his pictures of traction engines, the warden invited me up to his flat to see some more. He didn't say what it was he thought I would like to see some more of, however, until we arrived in the flat, when he ushered me into his bedroom and gave me some picture books to look at. I told him that they didn't seem to be a patch on the traction engines, made my excuses, and left, never to return until I heard that he, too, had been dismissed from his post.

We were initially bemused when Lt Clack-Quine arrived on the camp, because he was the spitting image of Corporal Stephenson, the medical orderly. At first, we thought that Corporal Stephenson had been miraculously promoted, but eventually got it sorted out. Sorting out was hastened by Schoolie Porter going into the medical room and finding – as he thought – Corporal Stephenson lying on the bed. 'Get up you skiving bastard' roared Schoolie Porter. 'I'm very sorry, Sergeant,' replied Lt Clack-Quine weakly, 'but I'm not feeling very well.'

Demobbed, Schoolie Porter, that son of the soil, went off to his agricultural college, and Christmas approached. It was inevitable that we should produce some sort of Christmas entertainment, and that I should be involved with scriptwriting and acting. Captain Taylor came to see how we were getting on since, knowing the team, there was obviously some possibility of gentle censorship being needed. Having seen what was going on, he was more concerned about the chaotic production than the script, and immediately offered his wife to take charge. We were very glad of this; and we were able to present a smooth evening's entertainment.

However, the full script had to be vetted by the adjutant and the only fault that he was able to find with it was in a sketch where an actor had to bring in something or other and put it down on stage. 'Not there, you fool,' was the line following this deed. We were severely taken to task. 'It's very bad form to call someone a fool on the stage' expostulated the adjutant. It was the first we'd heard of that. 'How would you like the line altered?' we asked. '"Oh, don't put it there you clot" would be all right' said the adjutant. We were glad that this was the only thing wrong with our script: we had thought that much more would have suffered the blue pencil. But we were vastly amused by the idea that there was some kind of thespian embargo on the word 'fool' and wrote in an extra sketch with an adjutant who exited saying: 'Come on chaps, there's gooseberry clot for lunch!'

Goodbye to all that

As soon as *Fantasy That*, the Christmas play, was over I came home on leave for a fortnight – which was odd, because I was due to be demobbed in the middle of February. The food on the Red Train was of the same standard as it had been on the way out but, as promised, it seemed to have deteriorated.

I had never been away from home for so long before, and so we had a belated Christmas lasting for quite some time before I retraced my steps for my last, and very short, stint in Germany. The last two or three weeks were spent in handing over to my successor, counting the books in the regimental library, packing all my acquisitions into a huge wooden case and taking it to Köln (only to find that the station was shut on Tuesday afternoons), and saying goodbye. Then back to Beaconsfield, the HQ of the RAEC whence I had set out the previous May.

Those of us who had been dispersed at that time had promised ourselves that we would have a grand demob reunion dinner at the *White Hart*, but it went off at half cock because we were all rather short of money. However, we did have some sort of celebration before our final early breakfast and return to civvy street.

Our last journey together – on the London underground – was marred by the disappearance of Adair's bag. Now Adair, known as Robin, had been in charge of Hut 28 at Beaconsfield during our training. He was somewhat authoritarian, especially when in charge of the hut, and had got it into his head that I disliked him because of his strict control. In fact, I thought that he had done the job very well and didn't dislike him at all. So when we remet at Beaconsfield, we each went out of our ways to be nice to the other, because neither of us liked feeling misunderstood. I was travelling comparatively light on that last morning, so I offered to help the overloaded Adair with his luggage as a gesture of friendship, and he allowed me to carry one of his kit-bags on the Circle Line. And, of course, when we got off, I forgot to pick it up. He exploded: 'You did it on purpose; you've never liked me since I was in charge of the hut; you just offered to carry it so that you could leave it on the train, *etc, etc.*' What could I say? I offered to help him retrieve the bag, but in vain: 'You've done enough already – get out of my sight.' Well, at least I didn't miss *my* train home and for all I know Robin and his kit-bag are still chasing one another round and round on the Circle Line.

. . . And that was really my last contact with the army. Some time after, I received an official letter asking me to pack all my kit into kit-bags, attach the labels provided, and take it to the station so that it could return to its home. They said I could keep various things – they didn't want the socks, pyjamas and towels back, for example – and I could buy the boots and greatcoat if I wished. So I kept everything I wanted and sent the rest off. After some time I received another official communication informing me that the packages had never arrived but, since I was able to prove that I had sent them, that was the end of that. Perhaps they, too, are going round and round on the Circle Line.

79 — *The Old House, Histon, from a painting by Elizabeth Smith.*

Part 4 : HISTON 1955–1993

The Old House

In the spring of 1954, Father saw a small, private advertisement in the *Cambridge Daily News* (as it was then) for The Old House, Histon. Colonel Lovelace had died and, having decided that the house was too large for her and her two sons, his widow sought to sell it privately.

The Old House is of red brick, built in about 1485 (according to some experts) and standing in a third of an acre in the heart of a village three miles from Cambridge. With enormous character, and ample room to stand motor cars, it was just what Father wanted – a little overpriced at £5,000, said the surveyor, 'but worth it if it particularly appeals'. And, of course, it did – to both my parents.

80 — *The Hall at The Old House in the days when it was occupied by Mr Brown, an antiquarian bookseller (picture from his catalogue).*

It took several months to organise everything and move in – indeed the move was not finally complete until just before I was demobbed on 17 February 1955.

For the numerous journeys back and forth – and possibly as an economy measure – Father had acquired an old Renault in faded red with the radiator behind the engine and hence the old slopy Renault bonnet. It wasn't really his type of vehicle as far as its style was concerned, but it was unusual so that made it all right.

The spring of 1955 gave place to summer; long, hot and halcyon. There were many tasks to carry out at The Old House; there was an extensive range of outbuildings needing benches, shelves and so on. There was a putative priest's hide to be explored, a trapdoor to be cut from the front landing to the loft, places still to be found for many of the things brought over from 142.

I devoted a lot of time to sound recording, and trying to become a jazz pianist, and spent many weekends going to London to visit friends who had migrated thence (Dave Rivett was becoming a dentist, for example).

Things of course had now changed. I had left the family at the beginning of 1953 as a schoolboy (albeit a 19-year-old one!) and had returned two years later as a grown up. I had been earning £5/15/6d a week as a National Service Sergeant, and had no way of matching – or bettering – that unless I got a job.

So amid the considerable pleasure-seeking of 1955 I returned to work for Ray Woodman the cabinet maker, but he had one or two other people by that time and there wasn't enough work to sustain me for long.

I went to see Dr Marsh, the father of a long-time school friend, who was in charge of the Research Department at that venerable institution the Cambridge Instrument Company (known in the town as 'The Scientific') and he took me on at 36.1d (15.042p) per hour. Most days I went back and forth in Lady C; occasionally in the Silver Ghost, when the day's wages hardly covered the cost of petrol.

One thing I never fathomed was where Father got his cars from, or where they went to. In much the same way as people used to bring stray cats to the Old House hoping for a good home (Father having over the years turned from strong indifference to domestic pets into a cat lover) so, I suspect, any garage finding itself lumbered with an unusual and unwanted car would give him a call. Generally, Father would buy a new (to him) car without telling Ma first. When he brought home his latest 4-wheeled friend he was faced with having to tell her about it. But he didn't really need to since he would saunter in, two fingers rubbing inside his collar and a particular look on his face.

Ma dreaded to think what car he was after when he disappeared without saying where he was going. Sometimes he would 'do a deal' on the spot by selling the car he went off in and driving home in the new one. I think he felt that if a new car suddenly appeared, people might not notice – and cars seemed to come and go to such an extent that one was never sure if a vehicle was fresh in or if it had been there for some time and one hadn't noticed. It would not have been prudent to ask.

Father compounded the mischief through his belief that, if you get one, you should try and get another for spares. The result of this was very often that the spare vehicle might lack some vital piece for the very reason that that piece was in demand. In the end, therefore, the spares turned into a collection of durable parts that no one would ever want because they never wore out.

In order to even up the finances spent on Father's cars, Ma would take an annual holiday in Italy or Sicily with her friend Teddy Edwards. This was probably the one week in the year she forgot about having a garden full of cars – though she was no doubt fearful of what new vehicle she would be collected in on her return.

Queens' College

On 5 October term began; I went 'up' to Queens' and found myself in digs with landparents Stan and Edna Nixon at 2 Union Road; it was very cold, and the lavatory was at the end of the garden. I was reading Natural Sciences – Chemistry, Zoology and Botany – more by accident than design; I had laid the foundations of that course when I was 14, and now I was 22. The grown-upness of being an Education Corps sergeant, and the freedom of the summer, had thoroughly upset my equilibrium and I was desperately unhappy.

One day as I was cycling along, I spotted Father progressing majestically and slowly in a cream 8-litre Bentley in favour at the time, off to get another pile of 'perishing books'.

I wanted to talk to him, and tell him all about it. I chased after him as he made his majestic way to Queen Anne Terrace, and there unburdened my woes. I said that I wanted to change my course, but since I hadn't thought it through I couldn't at that stage explain that I really wanted to read Mechanical Sciences.

When I'd managed to work that out, I found that Archie Brown, Director of Studies for Mechanical Science at Queens', would have none of it. I soldiered on until Easter 1957 and then left. Everyone was bitterly disappointed – including me, but I knew what I was going through.

In my second year I had rooms in College – T1, Fisher Court, now converted to the Porters' Lodge. I shared with Dick Marston, who subsequently bought the cream 8-litre Bentley from Father. Lady C was with me one week end; I was woken by a porter early on the Sunday morning suggesting that I should move her as she was blocking the Mathematical Bridge. It was obvious who had put her there; there had been a Rugby Club dinner the previous evening, and one of the revellers had inadvertently left his kit on the seat. He visited T1 on numerous occasions of growing desperation trying to retrieve his kit; I would hide in the bedroom, while Dick would feed some complex but spurious information on where I might be found. After a few weeks I relented, and let him have it back.

81 — Brother-in-law Rin (D Rintoul Booth) with the cream 8-litre Bentley SM8794 which Father owned from September 1952 to February 1956, when he sold it to Dick Marston, my room-mate at Queens'.

At the Old House, Father was finding – as always – that the garage section of the outbuildings wasn't big enough to accommodate all the vehicles. The garden needed rearranging as well, and various hedges and bushes gradually disappeared to make room for cars, and the manoeuvring of cars.

Eventually, he bought a quantity of railway sleepers, some joists from the magnificent house which was being demolished to make way for the new Parkside Police Station, and a quantity of corrugated asbestos, and built a carport big enough for four large cars. In spite of this, the lawn began to fill up with cars as well.

During my first term Judith, Rin and their mother returned from Australia after four years. The first thing Judith did after arriving in this country again was to ring me. What a thrill! She came to live in Cambridge, and after a few weeks we agreed to get married. The engagement took place in Dale's Sports Hearse in Wilberforce Road – according to the circumstances, the story of the proposal is either 'in a Rolls-Royce' or 'in a hearse'.

The Rolls-Royce Phantoms

The two Rolls-Royces for whom I felt the most affection were SD and NN. There were, however, others – the complete set (up to 1939) in fact.

The Phantom I was a bit of a wreck; she had belonged to the Duke of Bedford but had lately been used as a breakdown truck. Father nicknamed her Jagannatha (a Sanskrit word meaning 'Lord of the World' (Vishnu) – from which the word Juggernaut is derived).

82 — The Rolls-Royce New Phantom named Jagannatha *by Father. She had been painted primrose yellow and used as a breakdown truck.*

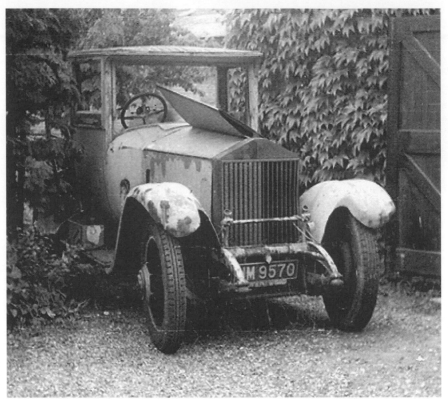

83 — Jagannatha *again. I'm not sure whether or not she was complete, but she never ran on the road and was eventually sold for spares.*

84 — *The chassis of the Rolls-Royce New Phantom (later to become Phantom I when the Phantom II was introduced). PI was produced from May 1925 and 'departs from the hitherto stereotype six-cylinder side-by-side valve engine, and adopts the push-rod operated overhead valve design.' This was chosen after 'exhaustive tests with the latest engine innovations, including a twelve-cylinder Vee-type engine, a "straight eight" and a supercharged unit, but after several years of experiment it was decided to adopt the six-cylinder overhead valve type.'*

85 — *The offside of the Rolls-Royce Phantom power unit showing the dual ignition system (magneto under the steering column, coil behind the radiator).*

86 — *The nearside of the Rolls-Royce Phantom power unit showing the manifolds and carburettors. The main carburettor is of Rolls-Royce design and has two jets and an automatic air valve. A separate small carburettor 'ensures easy and positive starting when the engine is cold'.*

The maximum engine speed of the Silver Ghost is 2,250rpm, and of the New Phantom 2,750rpm. At 2,250rpm the Phantom engine gives 33% more power than that of the Ghost, and the RAC rating (43.3hp) is 10% lower than that of the Ghost. The bore of the Phantom engine is 4.25″ (108mm) and the stroke 5.5″ (139.7mm); the capacity is about 7,960cc.

The Phantom II EU4229 was a different kettle of fish – long, sleek and black it went like the clappers and I drove it many miles, though the most memorable few yards were on a right-angled bend (now ironed out) which used to lie in wait notoriously between Cambridge and Newmarket. How remarkably the Phantom II held the road.

87 — *The Phantom II EU4288 on the lawn at the Old House. On the left is the rear of the Siddeley Special; on the right the rear of the Maybach (both of whom we will meet later).*

It was in EU that I experienced one of my closest shaves ever. We had all been to see Annie Baxter who had lived next door to my parents in Wanstead when they were first married and *persona non grata* with Uncle Edwin. I was driving quite fast through Epping Forest, and approaching a cross roads. Suddenly, there were cars in the middle of the road waiting to turn one way and the other, and other cars coming out of the side roads – I can picture it now, as I see myself stepping on the gas and sailing through the middle of it all like an intricately-choreographed Keystone Kops scene. Whether any of the passengers noticed, I never asked.

Talking of sailing through, there was a mysterious happening once when Father was driving along Newmarket Road and a black dog stepped off the pavement and started to trot across to the other side. Most people would have applied the anchors, but not Father – he just drove on as if nothing was happening. The odd thing was that the dog seemed to time its arrival so that the car passed unscathingly over it – it entered between the front wheels, and left between the offside wheels – and continued to the other side of the road. 'Did you see *that*?' asked Father. 'It seemed to pass through the car like a spook!' Perhaps it was that ghostly Fenland canine Black Shuck astray from his usual haunts.

The Phantom III EXW488 was a truly beautiful motor car, powered by a silent V12, and probably the most luxurious vehicle Father ever owned. The last time I saw it was in 1960 from the bay window of my upstairs office in Histon Road. It was being driven by none other than CJ Bendall, and it was far from silent as it went past. In fact, CJ had just bought it from Father and when he got it home rang up in high dudgeon to complain that the engine had deteriorated horrifically during the journey and now needed a complete overhaul 'which will be very, very expensive'. Father had had no idea that the engine was on the brink of collapse, and the car had sounded as silent as ever when it left Histon, so it was all jolly hard cheese.

88 — Possibly the finest car Father ever had – the 1938 Phantom III. Standing by it is Robert Yates, chiefly known for sleeping with a loaded revolver under his pillow, a habit he had acquired in Africa. Robert's car is the Standard CEK976. Part of a collection of horse-drawn vehicles is seen on the lawn.

The Rolls 20s

Father had at least two Rolls 20/25s. First there was the cream one that had belonged to a Mr Hart, and sported a silver hart mascot. Then came the black one (MZ2914) which was a little shoddy, affording an excuse to repaint it in yellow with green trimmings. It was about the time that the film *The Yellow Rolls-Royce* came out (1961), giving rise to a good deal of predictable comment.

89 — *Barry attending to the 1930 Rolls 20 before it went yellow. Note Father's titanic carport.*

The Dennis Fire Engine – EW3258

Father went to Les Rich and, seeing a Dennis Fire Engine, complete with ladders and everything, decided he'd like to buy it. Unfortunately (no, quite the opposite) Rich ruled that he 'was not allowed' to sell the ladders so, when it arrived, the fire engine was somewhat emasculated.

On the back was a wonderful pump driven from the engine via an auxiliary gearbox. We took the pump off and wondered what we could do with the power take-off facility. Then – a brilliant idea – what about turning it into a circular saw? I bought an two-foot saw blade and an arbor and rigged it up in place of the pump. The angle-irons from an old bed frame provided a track for a wheeled traverse for passing the wood to be sawn smoothly across the blade. Not without trepidation, we started the engine and ran it up. It was rather frightening, but it cut through tree-trunks like butter. In no time there were enough logs to keep the open fire in the hall at the Old House going for some weeks. (That fire hardly ever went out in nearly 40 years.) As an exercise it was a complete success, but with my experience of working for Ray Woodman I was well aware of the dangers of circular saws and what could happen if the saw had a mind to jam in the cut.

Father used the Fire Engine as a runabout for a little while, a great head-turner as he drove through the streets of Cambridge. However, it was very heavy to drive (no power steering) and very exposed to the elements, so the novelty soon wore off.

90 — *Father and Ma looking happy on the Dennis fire engine.*

91 — *The Firehouse Five + 3 one summer evening in 1956. On the ground (left) is an unknown trombonist. The trombonist on the fire engine is Roy Rubinstein and standing precariously on a collapsing box behind him is Mike Payne on bass. The late 'Wooden' Dud Clews (whose name lives on in the Coventry-based Dud Clews Big Band) is sitting on the circular saw blade, with his trumpet obscuring Chris Cook on clarinet and pointing at pianist Rod Dale (who couldn't get his instrument on to the vehicle). I don't know the name of the standing guitarist; the one seated is Laurence O'Toole (Lar).*

92 — Elements of the band on the lawn before someone thought of climing on to the fire engine (left). Note the Brown Hillman ER8045 in the background.

In the fifties, Devi Das Argawala arrived from India and found a job on a building site, working all hours and snatching sleep behind doors propped against a wall. By dint of hard work, he set up a print shop, Maxspeed (Mill Road), opened one of the first Indian restaurants in Cambridge (The Kismet, Northampton Street), and became a respected business man and property owner.

Mr Whitelegg used to approach the Dales every summer to produce some interesting vehicles as an attraction for the Coleridge School fête he organised; Lady C became a well-known visitor and, in due time, the Fire Engine. One year, the Fire Engine and 'Professor' Argawala came together when the former acted as a travelling platform for the latter to demonstrate feats of strength, bending iron bars in the manner of an Indian fakir, and eating razor blades and light bulbs (don't try this at home, children).

The career of the Fire Engine came to an end when Mr Spencer the Customs and Excise man knocked on the door of the Old House. It was I who answered the door, and had to deal with him. He had heard that we had a fire engine on which purchase tax had not been paid. The tenor of his argument was that vehicles such as ambulances, fire engines and the like were exempt from purchase tax, but if they were later sold to someone who did not qualify for such exemption, then that purchaser would be liable to pay purchase tax. The tenor of *my* argument was that, since the vehicle had been registered before purchase tax was introduced, it couldn't have been not paid, so we were not liable. Mr Spencer went away.

In due course a letter came setting out the case and stating the amount of purchase tax due. Father decided not to argue the toss – I think he was glad of a face-saving way of giving up the vehicle – so it was driven to an orchard he acquired for a short time and may still be there for all I know.

93 — *The fire engine ends its days in the Secret Garden; brother-in-law Barry Puttick relaxing after some orchard-related task. The teeth of the saw blade are seen menacingly behind him. The ends of the track for the sliding table protrude on the left.*

The Hillmans – ER8045 & ER5955

In the mid-50s, we acquired two Hillman Heavy 12s. The 'Brown Hillman' ER8045 came first – a good solid car with the usual 4-cylinder side valve engine and beautiful leather upholstery. The back of the front bench seat could be adjusted with a bolt each side which screwed into a choice of holes in a strip; take the bolts out altogether and the seat went down flat, turning the car into a bed. It was in this that Steve and I went on a camping tour of Cornwall in 1956. By a dispensation of providence, the front door hinged at the front, and the back door at the back, so we were able to augment the somewhat cramped space – if it was a bed, it could be nothing else – by an awning on a frame supported by the open doors.

ER8045 was great fun to trundle about in, with the straight-tooth crash gearbox that makes such a delightful musical noise in the lower ratios. In London, one day, I was shooting up Shoot Up Hill NW2 when there was a sudden loss of oomph (or, perhaps gain of 00mph) caused, we found on inspection, by a broken half-shaft.

I arranged with the Cricklewood Garage to collect and store the car while I found another half-shaft, and returned home by train.

With the help of *Exchange & Mart* I located a breaker's yard in Gipsy Hill which had just what I wanted – it was just a matter of getting it out. After many a phone call: ''Allo, *YES*. Con 'ere . . .' I persuaded Con to get round to extracting the half-shaft and to send it over to the Cricklewood Garage. That part of the exercise was £2/10/-.

My phoning now turned to Cricklewood, to persuade them to install the half-shaft, which they eventually did. Down to London by train, and to Cricklewood with Dave Rivett. Recovery, storage and repair came to £3/17/6d. I paid and we were making ready to drive away when I couldn't find the receipt (though I don't know why I wanted it). I sent Dave in to see if it was in the office. He came back empty-handed, but added a phrase to our language: 'He says you must have put it in one of your numerous pockets'.

Then, across the road from the Old House, appeared David Bentinck with a used car lot, and a slightly earlier Hillman Heavy 12, the smoky-blue ER5955. Indignant that he couldn't haggle it below £17/10/-, Father bought this car because he'd already got one.

Our 1956 Cornwall trip inspired me to design a folding caravan for the summer of 1957. A central section on wheels provided a wardrobe and kitchen, and there was a fold-out bed on an ingenious ambivalent quadrilateral principle on each side, the whole consisting in a canvas-covered wooden frame. The wheels came from Ray Woodman's trailer, and served very well. Our only mishap was about three miles from the start of the journey when one of the nuts holding the axle fell off, and the caravan body jumped to an angle – luckily held by the other nut. A new nut and a spanner, and we were soon on our way again.

The Hillmans did a great job, but their brakes were a bit uncertain because the curvature of the brake-shoes was not quite the same as that of the drums. I occasionally dream that I'm driving a vehicle – not necessarily a Hillman, though sometimes it is – suffering from this fault. How odd the workings of the human mind.

94 — *Hillman ER5955 and the folding caravan in Mr Whitcomb's garden at Board Cross House, Shepton Mallet. The inside of the door of Mr Whitcomb's lavatory for campers' use was covered with helpful information. The list of places of interest memorably included 'Rock of Ages Fame'.*

95 — *Steve with Dartmoor ponies*

96 — The folding caravan at Harlyn Bay, Cornwall, ready for use, Steve standing by. Among other utensils, the kitchen section contains a whistling kettle standing on our faithful old primus stove, no stranger to Cornwall. There is one bed on each side into which the sleeper had to crawl, long before the modern Japanese hotel design.

97 — The folding caravan at Harlyn Bay, waiting to move off. We had some trouble with secure catches to keep the body frames shut, and the ropes helping to perform that function are to be seen front and back. We went to Harlyn Bay because Mike Payne and his parents had been going there to camp every summer since time began, and had oft extolled its virtues. Moreover, it was comforting to meet people one knew when a long way from home.

On leaving Queens' in 1957, I went along to the Cambridge Instrument Company to see if they'd take me on permanently; unfortunately – but understandably – they had no vacancy to suit me.

Thinking round all the people I knew, I went to see Mr Townsend who was MD of Cathodeon Ltd in Cambridge, a member of the Pye Group, which manufactured camera tubes, glass-to-metal seals and aircraft crash-switches. As the parent of two teenage boys talking to someone who had been a teenager much more recently than he had, Mr Townsend mused upon his sons and their inexplicable activities for an hour or two and then offered me a job as a spade-and-bucket chemist for about £6 per week. I rented a house in Cambridge with two friends, and my vintage motoring days were more or less over.

Goodbye Lady C

After I'd moved on to the Hillmans, and then into Cambridge, Lady C was sadly abandoned. Dick 'Bygones' Joice of Anglia Television came to make a programme about the Old House, and Father, and his cars, and suggested he might buy Lady C for his Holkham Hall Bygones Collection – where she still lives. Father felt it would help to clear the lawn, and off she went with a goodly pile of motorcycle parts thrown in – £50 the lot.

98 — Lady C and friends on the Old House lawn shortly before her departure. Father is attending to the Phantom II; in the foreground is the Rolls 20 before it went yellow,

99 — Lady C's front-axle geometry always made her look a bit skew-whiff unless the wheels were straight ahead.

100 — *Another view of Lady C, showing also the rear ends of the Rolls 20 and the Siddeley Special.*

101 — *Lady C's sad condition shows as she sits on Dick Joice's lorry; although her side panels were aluminium, the dickey-seat panel was steel.*

The Morris Minor

Steve was seventeen in 1958 and of course she wanted to learn to drive, so Father obtained a Morris Minor for her.

'Having grown up close to cars and watching Father drive for years it didn't appear too difficult,' she says. 'The greatest problem was the steering – it seemed to go one way or the other and it was not very easy to get it to go in a straight line.'

Steve was keeping a horse at Haslingfield at the time, and this made an ideal opportunity for some driving practice. I accompanied her on many journeys back and forth. We both recall the memorable moment when she took a blind corner on the wrong side of the road, fortunately with no dire physical consequences, though she has never felt particularly keen on driving since.

102 — *The Calormeter, a day and night reading radiator thermometer.*

103 — Steve at Frinton-on-Sea.

104 — Steve's Morris Minor – the car in which she learned to drive. It ran very well, but the fabric body began to rot as the poor car stood by the greenhouse. Neither of us knows whence the car came, nor whither it went.

105 — *The Morris Minor handbook suggests that all four wheels should be raised from the ground when you adjust the brakes. Balancing on bricks as shown, however, can only be described as a foolhardy enterprise; perhaps the company thought that it would bring it closer to its typical audience.*

The Maybach – VUU92

Wilhelm Maybach was the Daimler engineer who designed the original Mercedes, so named after the eldest daughter of Emil Jellinek, who was the local agent for Daimler cars as well as being the Austro-Hungarian consul in Nice. (Nice work!) Maybach then joined Zeppelin to produce airship engines, and then aero engines in general. He started building cars in 1921.

Father acquired an SW38 Maybach towards the very end of the 50s. Built in 1939, it was the car which the West German Chancellor, Dr Adenauer, used during his state visit to England in 1958. It was shipped over to enhance Dr Adenauer's prestige; £2,000 was spent on reconditioning and strengthening the body (*ie* making it bullet-proof).

Described as 'a Germanic box of tricks' the Maybach had a 6-cylinder 3.8 litre engine, vacuum gear change, eight forward speeds and four reverse: 'The low-ratio set is for mountainous country; the other for flat country'.

Like other cars of this period, it came, moved about ponderously for a time, and then went unremarked.

106 — *The Maybach in 1961 – 'its spare tyres are carried in wing compartments' remarked the* Cambridge Evening News, *presumably at a loss for anything else to say.*

107 — *The rear compartment of the Maybach. Note the rudimentary seatbelt.*

108 —*The Maybach SW38 chassis.*

109 —*The Maybach SW38 engine and gearbox.*

110 — *'A Germanic box of tricks.'*

111 — *Heavy engineering – the Maybach front suspension.*

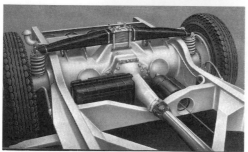

112 — *The Maybach rear axle – reminiscent of a rail traction unit.*

The Siddeley Special – BAH400

Armstrong Siddeley (no hyphen) came into being in 1919 when Siddeley-Deasy merged with the car manufacturing division of the Northumbrian engineering and shipbuilding giant Armstrong-Whitworth. Though described as clumsy and ungainly, the post-first-war Armstrong Siddeleys were nevertheless described (by their manufacturer) as 'cars of aircraft quality' – just because their engines came from the Armstrong aero-engine manufacturing plant.

113 — The 1938 Siddeley Special. The thermostatically-operated louvres conceal a flat radiator core – cheaper to manufacture than the earlier pointed core. The 6-cylinder 88.9 x 133.4mm engine had a capacity of 4960cc.

The six-cylinder 12hp model – along with a 10, 20 and 30 – ran throughout the thirties but, although one feels that the marque sought to emulate the upmarket image of the Rolls-Royce, it never made it. A better power–weight ratio, and a proper gearbox (rather than the Wilson preselector which made the military tank possible) might have helped. My account of our experiences with KV6744 (p30) bears this out.

The 5-litre 6-cylinder Siddeley Special – drawing on aero-engine practice, but still with a Wilson preselector gearbox – was launched at the 1932 Motor Show, and 140 cars were sold during the four years of its life. Father had two of them: the one depicted, BAH400, was registered in May 1936. The maximum speed was quoted as 90mph. I can testify from travelling in the late forties in the Mansfields' 1936 Wolesley that, on the roads of the time, 90mph seemed very fast indeed. However, I don't think I ever drove, or rode in, this car.

According to *The Autocar* (7 June 1935), the Siddeley Special illustrates the way in which 'scientific research is constantly helping to make a commercial possibility today out of yesterday's dreams. When the Siddeley Special design reached production stage rather over two years ago it represented the achievement of an ideal: the ideal of a car with perfect carriage comfort and good manners, but further possessed of a latent road performance to equal that of any so-called sports model – a large car, powerful but light because of its special construction, and able to travel fast and easily over long distances if required.'

A new light alloy, Hiduminium, developed jointly by Rolls-Royce and John Siddeley's High Duty Alloys Ltd was used extensively in the engine; the densest parts of the engine were the steel valves and crankshaft.

114 — Offside of Siddeley Special engine – distributor and plugs.

115 — Near side of Siddeley Special engine-inlet and exhaust manifold. The engine enjoyed hydraulic tappets before Rolls-Royce fitted them to the Phantom III.

The Decline

In 1932, shortly after marrying my mother, Father had suffered Dietl's crisis – a kidney becomes detached and, in shifting, kinks the ureter, which is not pleasant – resulting, in his case, in removal of the kidney.

Some ten years later, he was found to have a stone in the remaining kidney, and had to have it cut out (just like Mr Pepys, except that Father had an anaesthetic). As a treat, I was allowed to visit him in Addenbrooke's Hospital on Christmas Day; my abiding memory is the depressingly dim lighting in the ward (no doubt all these huge windows were blacked out) and sticky juice from fruit salad spilling from an unsuitably profiled plate on to my lap and into my shoes.

Notwithstanding this, Father was a very active man, but the strain on his single kidney began to tell as he reached his 60s, and he became quite lethargic, spending a lot of time dozing on the sofa. His depressed state may have been exacerbated by his reaching the age at which some ill-advised palm-reading busybody at King's had told him he would die. He got through that year, but seemed to me never to be the same again.

So Father soldiered on, taking a whole armamentarium of medicaments, resting on the sofa, getting and preparing fish for the cats, and going out and wrestling with the enormous Daimler batteries which seemed to be a constant source of trouble.

The Daimlers

By now the lawn at The Old House was clear; Rolls-Royces, Maybach and Siddeley Special had gone, and their place had been taken by three DE36 straight-eight Daimlers.

Daimler is, of course, a venerable old name in motoring; it was Gottlieb Daimler who pinned his faith (rightly) on the high-speed, high-compression-ratio engine, whereas the other early name of note, Carl Benz, favoured the huge single cylinder wherefrom each explosion shudders the vehicle forward another few feet. FR Simms bought British rights in Daimler's engine patents in 1891; the Daimler Motor Company in Coventry came into being in 1896.

In 1900, the Prince of Wales bought a 6hp Daimler, which established the marque as the royal choice. During the reign of Edward VII, Daimler built a 4-cylinder 3.3 litre and a 6-cylinder 10.4 litre, both with poppet-valves. In 1908, the Company acquired the right to manufacture the Knight sleeve-valve engine – the 'Silent Knight'. In 1910 Daimler was absorbed into the BSA (Birmingham Small Arms) Group, and until November 1919 produced a selection of mechanical items needed for warfare – from aircraft, through tanks and cars, to shells. The Company continued to supply cars to the Royal family. In

1926, Chief Engineer Lawrence Pomeroy brought out a V12 engine, followed by the fluid flywheel in 1930 which, in conjunction with the Wilson pre-selector gearbox, provided a smooth and easy drive. In the mid-1930s, poppet-valve engines improved and the relatively complex sleeve-valve engine was dropped with the introduction of a 4.6-litre straight eight engine – the design that powered Father's three Daimlers.

116 — *The DE36 Daimler chassis.*

I don't know what order they appeared in, but their multiplying was a consequence of Father's belief that you should always have more than one of anything – or possibly if it's cheap enough you ought to buy it (whatever it is).

The DE36 Straight-Eight chassis was 18´6˝ long and weighed nearly two tons. The 85 x 120mm engine had a volume of 5,460cc and produced 150bhp at 3,600rpm. The fluid flywheels and preselector boxes always gave one a feeling of not quite knowing where one was.

The chief sources of worry were the batteries – two very heavy-duty 6-volt batteries connected in series to give the standard 12 volts. Father was always lifting them out and taking them somewhere to be rebuilt or overhauled, and they frequently seemed to let him down. With three cars providing six batteries he could generally find a working pair, but I don't think he ever had them all serviceable at the same time. The strain of lifting them in and out doubtless contributed to his heart problems.

In his last letter to me, Father described the Daimlers in the hope that I could help him to 'get rid' of them:

The 3 Daimlers =

   1. Eaden Lilley's Hearse 1948, brakes need attention, battery u/s, cost £200 – say £100?

   2. The Daimler Works car 1946 [FVC321], new engine 1961, battery u/s, cost £800 with new king pins – say £600?

   3. The Daimler said to have been made for KGVI (according to the Birmingham Branch of the Old Daimler Co) *c*1950 [LXD342], battery u/s, needs new king pins cost £600 – say £400? . . . Anybody who would take the 3 *as they stand* can have them for £1,000. I think we want a lighthearted advert – they might be described as 'fun cars' . . .

Clearly king pins were second only to batteries as sources of trouble.

117 —*The Daimler DE36 works car of 1946; new engine and king pins 1961.*

118 — *DE36 Straight Eight Daimler, said to have been built for King George VI.*

119 — *View in the rear (passengers') compartment of the DE36. In this body there are two occasional seats (one folded away) and a magazine rack. King George's Daimler had a cocktail cabinet. Note the electrically-operated glass partition.*

120 — *Another view of the DE36 rear interior – a good deal more plush than the Maybach.*

The Ford Galaxie

Father's last car – which made up a foursome with the Daimlers – was a Ford Galaxie. It had originally been registered as TWA1 and used by TransWorld Airlines to ferry VIPs to and from airports to London. It was very large and powerful and automatic, and it spelt the end of his motoring when he either stepped on the wrong pedal or failed to step on the right one – whatever happened, the result was that the car leapt forward and struck a wall, which stopped it, thank goodness. It caused extensive damage to the wall, to the car, and to Father's confidence. He never drove again. By the time I heard about this incident and rushed over to see him, the car had been removed to Horseheath to be repaired. Father's last letter, quoted above, with all its Daimler description, doesn't mention the Galaxie.

The end

In a memoir of his Addenbrooke's days, Father had written: 'Old men die at three in the morning' and he bore out the truth of that statement on 14 April 1972 – except that at 63 he wasn't that old. It fell to me to dispose of the three Daimlers and the Ford Galaxie. As usual, there were wiseacres queuing up to tell me how valuable these cars must be and how they'd be snapped up as soon as I advertised them. I didn't think getting rid of them would be at all easy, and in fact it took weeks and weeks (on and off). An undertaker – or perhaps he was a would-be undertaker – eventually took the hearse and FVC321, and a 'nice young man', so described by my mother, bought LXD342 for (I think) £325.

As for the Ford Galaxie, I don't know why it went to Horseheath for repair – perhaps the garage there was flavour of the month. I held little love for it, looking upon it as a deodand, and my mind is more or less blank on its fate – I can't even remember driving it home, though I know I did. Probably I sold it for somewhat less than the sum needed to settle the repair bill.

Mother died on 8 August 1993 and at last I was forced to undertake the task about which she had been nagging me gently on and off for years – clearing the outbuildings (not to mention the inbuildings). Some of the stuff had been moved over from 142 lock, stock and barrel almost 40 years before. Almost every nut and bolt, every curiously shaped piece of wood, every chunk of metal, carried some association or memory.

I gathered an ever-increasing pile of motor parts and found an enthusiastic dealer in autojumble who took it all away – he was particularly taken by the louvred sides of the Hispano-Suiza bonnet which had served as a shelf for nearly forty years. They had come from the car that provided OX 6934's second body, and the hinged top of the bonnet had made the mudguards for Lady C. Mr Autojumble drooled over a great mass of oil pipes complete with nuts and nipples from all manner of dismantled vehicles, and piles of magnetos, carburettors, manifolds and the rest. And the mystery cylinder block – for weeks after he would telephone me to see if I had any new ideas as to its possible identity.

Many things went, but many I've kept – unable to dispose of them, for to throw away tangible evidence of one's memories is, I think, to admit one's own mortality. But there's still time to sort it all out . . .

LIST OF VEHICLES ENCOUNTERED

A4281	Panhard et Levassor (*Le Papillon Bleu*)
AH242	Humberette
BAH400	Siddeley Special
BRB800	Bugatti
CE2082	Morris Bullnose
CF4994	Ford Model T
CF9516	Rover 8
DP6530	Cluley 10.4
DM270	Darracq
DX6300	Humber
EER451	Henderson motorcycle
ELB374	Fiat Tipolino
ER5955	Hillman Heavy 12
ER7000	Armstrong-Siddeley 20
ER7982	Swift
ER8045	Hillman Heavy 12
ER9402	Sunbeam
EU4228	Rolls-Royce Phantom II
EW1217	BSA mtorocycle
EW3258	Dennis fire engine
EXW488	Rolls-Royce Phantom III
EXY938	Wolseley
FVC321	Daimler DE36
GT8771	Bentley blower 4.5
GVB514	Rover 8 (Goods)
GY7850	Bentley 8-litre (alias JVE820)
HJ2903	Rudge-Multi motorcycle
HP7707	Rover 8
JVE820	Bentley 8-litre (alias GY7850)
KV6744	Armstrong-Siddeley 12
LB8229	Panhard et Levassor van
LXD342	Daimler DE36
M22	Panhard phaeton
ML2075	Star
MMG329	Bentley 8-litre
MZ2914	Rolls-Royce 20
NM9570	Rolls-Royce Phantom I
NN3740	Rolls-Royce Silver Ghost
OX6934	Bentley 4.5-litre
P4678	Minerva
PB6163	GWK

RF36	Sunbeam
SD6295	Rolls-Royce Silver Ghost
SM8794	Bentley 8-litre
T2523	motorcycle of unknown make
TWA1	Ford Galaxie
UV1928	Bentley Speed Six
VE8473	Rolls-Royce Phanton
VF2315	Swift
VUU92	Maybach
VX4316	Rover 10
XU1495	Talbot
XV6688	Bentley 4.5-litre
XW7735	Vauxhall
YB6694	Clyno
YF9093	Bentley Big Six/Speed Six
YO9550	Humber
YP8563	Lorraine-Dietrich Silken Six
YX9221	Bugatti

INDEX

Figures in bold refer to illustrations

Branch, Jack: 73

Brooke, David: **62–65**, 74+; on Life with a Cluley 77+

Bryant, Sir Arthur: 6

BSA motorcycle: **22**; carries historic road-fund licence **24**

Bucknall, Leslie: 62

Bugatti Type 57: **44**

Bullnose Morris: 14, **15**,

Cambridge streets: Abbey Road 47; Belmont Place 41; Cam Road 44; Caroline Place 25; Chesterton Road 11+; **12**, 54, 77; Conduit Head Road   61; Corn Exchange 84; de Freville Avenue 26, 76; Devonshire Road 39; East Road 28; Elizabeth Way 11; Haig Road 11; Harvey Road 49; Hawthorn Way 17; Jesus Lane 47; King's Parade 58; Marlowe Road 31; Midsummer Common 38; Mill Road 118; Mitcham's Corner 20, 27; Northampton Street 118; Quayside 28; Queen Anne Terrace 29, 46; Rathmore Road 37; Regent Street **85**; Romsey Town 21; St Eligius Street 47; Tennis Court Road 47

Cambridge Cycle Company: 41

Cambridge Instrument Company: 108, 122

Cambridge School of Art: 89

Cambridge University Jazz Band: 54+

Campbell, Patrick: 80

caravan, folding: **94**, **96**, **97**, 120+

car breakers' yards: 13+, 120

Cathodeon Ltd, of Cambridge: 89, 123

Chamberlain, Neville: 11

Chappell: Edith 1+; Edwin (senior) 1+; Edwin (junior) *see* Uncle; H & Co **1**, 9+

142 Chesterton Road, Cambridge: 11, **12**, 54, 77

Clack-Quine, Lt: 104

Clarabelle, Grampound cow: **36**

Clews, Dudley, cornettist: **91**

Cluley 10.4: **60–65**; 72+; David Brooke on 77+

Clutton, Cecil: 61, **65**

Clyno 10: **41**, **65**

Cook, Christopher, clarinettist: **91**, **92**

Crosse, Tony, Henderson owner: 39

Crossley 20: 64

Daimler hearse, *memento mori*: 14

Daimler DE36: **116–119**, 132

Dale, Celia *neé* Hutchinson *see* Ma

Dale, Donald Alexander: *see* Father

Dale, Alexander Mayo: 1+

Dale, Rodney: born 9; moves to Cambridge 11; inventor, enjoys
 breakers' yards 13; bus enthusiast 14; enjoys 4.5-litre Bentley **11**,
 17+; transformer nightmare **13**; Father's driving instruction,
 Felixstowe holidays 24+; finds Tipolino cramped 29; recalls
 Jack's Hill 32; escapes poisoning 34; Big Six reunion **20**;
 motorcycling experiences 38+; acquires Lady C 42+; learns to
 drive 45+; passes test 48; Cornish trip 1951 49+; Bentley
 breaker, cactus breeder, discovers jazz 54; meets John Stanford
 56+; visits Alec Hodsdon, rides on *Le Papillon Bleu* 62+; drives
 Gardner-Serpollet 64; visits Norwich **52**; drives John Stanford's
 Crossley 64; finds a GWK 65; finds a Humberette 67; builds
 useless trailer 67+; enjoys Lorraine-Dietrich 68+; visits Norfolk
 Broads 75+; does the ton on an 8-litre Bentley 82; drives a
 Darracq for a week **72**, 84; drives Silver Ghost 86; works at
 Cathodeon 89; breaks wrist 90; enjoys National Service 91+;
 goes to Queens' College 109+; becomes engaged to Judith 110;
 breaks Hillman half-shaft, tours Cornwall again, designs and
 builds folding caravan 120+; leaves Queens' College 122; sells
 cars and autojumble 135+

Dale's Sports Hearse: sawn down 87; romantic setting 111

Darracq: **72**, 84

de Knyff, Chevalier René: 62

Delpine, Lily *see* Hutchinson, Lily

Dennis Fire Engine: acquired 116+; used **90, 91, 93**; abandoned 119

Duke, Richard: **31**

Dynamotor: **42**

East Boscombe (Pokesdown): 3

Eastern Counties Omnibus Company: 14

Eastern National Omnibus Company: 14

Ely, destination: 21

Emerson & Jayne (and the Magic Carpet): 13

Erskine, Robert: **52**

Father: in 1960 **Frontispiece**; when young 2; bored by Wagner 3; ditto
 by caterpillar 4; on the Humberette **4**; plays a horn **5**; rides a
 motorcycle **6**; pictured **8**; marries in secret 9; unused to business
 10; pursues PhD at King's College, Cambridge 11; teaches
 English at March, makes handbags, collects leather 13; becomes
 a tricyclist 15+, 89+; buys Bentley chassis and fits body 17+;
 chased by a hornet 22; takes old ladies to polls, collects petrol

coupons 23; revises driving skills 24+; driving mishaps 26; handsignals 28; owns Fiat momentarily 29; engraves tyres 30; buys Big Six Bentley 33; squashes watering can, extinguishes Big Six blaze 34; pushes difficult motorcycle 38; buys Lady C 42+; builds big top 43+, 74; accompanies RD on drives 45; explains Brushing Belco 48; discovers CJ Bendall 60; buys seized Phœnix 61; meets the Tampoes 61; meets David Brooke 77; acquires and re-registers 8-litre Bentley 80+; buys a Silver Ghost 85+; buys another 87+; breaks ankle at School of Art 89+; collects RD's belongings in Ghost 98; buys the Old House, Histon 107; buys another 8-litre Bentley **81**, 109; builds a carport 110; buys a New Phantom (Phantom I) **82**, **83**, 111; buys a Phantom II **87**, 114; buys a Phantom III **88**, 114; sells it 115; acquires Rolls 20s; buys a fire engine **90**, 116+; acquires Maybach **106**, 126+; acquires Siddeley Special **113–115**, 129+; renal problems 131; clears Lawn, but acquires Daimlers 131+; and a Ford Galaxie, and reaches the end of the road 135.

Hillman Heavy 12s: 120+

Hispano-Suiza: provides luggage grid 16; body for 4.5 Bentley 37; makes
  Rover mudguards **31**, 48, 135; Silver Ghost disguised as, or not
  as the case may be 87

Hodsdon, Alec: **50, 51**, 62+

Holkham Hall, Norfolk: 123

Howe, Mr Leslie, Darracq driver: 85

Hulme, John, coachbuilder: 33, 37

Humberette, Father on **4**; at Lavenham **54**

Hutchinson, Celia: *see* Ma

Hutchinson, George: marries 7; goes to war, remarries 8; supplies lighter
  fuel 18+

Hutchinson, Lily: and Maria Montessori **7**, 8+

Ingleton, Donald: 100

Ison's Garage *see* Smith, Tom

Jack's Hill Café: 32

Jagannatha: 111+

Jeffries, Mick: **32, 34, 35, 37**, 49+

Joice, Dick: 123+

Jones, Brennan: **40**, 55

Jones, Ieuan Lloyd, boogie pianist: 55

King & Harper (*alias* Sting & Sharper): 27

Kirkman, Sid: 31

kylin: 26

Lady C: catches fire 37; discovered 42+; worm & wheel rear axle drive
  26; TS engine **27**; LS engine **28**; bends front axle 46; nearside of
  engine **29**; underside **30**; early outing **31**; trip to Cornwall 49+,
  32–39; at Milton **40**; goes to battle 94+; leaves for Holkham Hall
  98–101

The Lane: 11, **62–65**

Langford, Mr, driving examiner: 48

Lawrence, DH: 42

Lea-Francis: 23

Lilliput: 80

Lister, George: 47

The Loft: 11

Lorraine-Dietrich Silken Six: **55–58**, 68+; seizes up 71; stork mascot **59**,
  72

Lovelace, Col: 107

Luckett, Richard: 5

Prince of Wales *later* King Edward VII: 62, 131
Puttick, Barry, *RD's brother-in-law*: **89**, **93**
Puttick, Steve: *see* Sister Steve
Queens' College: chosen 49; attended 109+; abandoned 122
RAC rating: 24
Rayner, Vic: chauffeur **11**, **12**, 24
Rayner, Lilian: **11**; **12**
Redex upper-cylinder lubricant: 28, 38, 61, 74
Reeve, John: **63**, **64**, 75+
Rich, Leslie A, car-breaker: described 13+, supplies Hispano-Suiza
      luggage grid 16, supplies Sunbeam body 17; supplies Rover
      Eight 42; supplies Rover parts **31**; supplies Dennis Fire Engine
      without ladders 116
Rivett, Dave: and the old Rolls 89; reports on numerous pockets 120
road-fund licence: comes into being 41+, **24**, **25**; from 8-litre Bentley
      before and after **66**
Rochester, 2nd Earl of, *Restoration poet*: 10
Rock of Ages Fame: 121
Roderick, Dr Henry, his Sunbeam: **47**
Roe, Roger: 49
Rolls-Royce: 1919 Silver Ghost **73**, 85+; the flick trick 87; starter sticks
      88+; New Phantom (Phantom I) **82–86**, 111+; Phantom II **87**;
      Phantom III **88**, 114; 20s **89**, 115+
Rooke, Harry: fits Sunbeam body 17+; actions recalled 68
Rover Eight *see* Lady C
Royal Naval College, Greenwich: 5, 7
Royce, Henry, his dual ignition system: 87
Rubinstein, Roy, trombonist: **91**
Rudge-Multi motorcycle: 38+; engine **23**
Salisbury, Ted, motor engineer: 44
Sallabank, Capt W: 95
Sangster, Robert, Rover Eight designer: 42
Scudamore Bros: 25
Secret Garden: **93**
Sewell, Mrs & Mrs Les, of Ashdon: 23
Shellactitis (-osis): 38, 79
Short, Tony: **40**, 54+; & his Sackdroppers: 54+
Shute, Nevil, motorcyclist: 38
Shuttleworth, Richard Ormond: 32
Siddeley Special: **113–115**, 129+